Computers in Education

A Research Bibliography

Richard A. Diem

Routledge
Taylor & Francis Group
Routledge Revivals

First published in 1988
by Garland Publishing Inc

This edition first published in 2018 by Routledge
2 Park Square, Milton Park, Abingdon, Oxon, OX14 4RN
and by Routledge
711 Third Avenue, New York, NY 10017

Routledge is an imprint of the Taylor & Francis Group, an informa business

Publisher's Note
The publisher has gone to great lengths to ensure the quality of this reprint but points out that some imperfections in the original copies may be apparent.

Disclaimer
The publisher has made every effort to trace copyright holders and welcomes correspondence from those they have been unable to contact.

A Library of Congress record exists under LCCN: 88023642

ISBN 13: 978-1-138-57424-3 (hbk)
ISBN 13: 978-0-203-70115-7 (ebk)
ISBN 13: 879-1-138-57426-7 (pbk)

Routledge Revivals

Computers in Education

Published in 1988, this bibliography focuses on four main areas; descriptions of the computer and its effects on human thinking and learning, computers in teaching situations, problems arising from the use of computers, and examinations of the future use of computers in education. Publications with relevant information are included, and in some cases studies have been annotated to provide more information on the citation.

The bibliography presents researchers with a listing of primary and secondary sources detailing the role of the computer in education from 1975 to 1986. Short term, as well as longitudinal studies are included, across all formats including articles, reviews, dissertations and books.

LIBRARY OF CONGRESS
Library of Congress Cataloging-in-Publication Data

Diem, Richard A.
Computers in education : a research bibliography / Richard A. Diem.
p. cm. — (The Garland bibliographies in contemporary education ; vol. 8) (Garland reference library of social science ; vol. 369)
Includes indexes.
ISBN 0–8240–8541–8 (alk. paper)
1. Education—United States—Data processing—Bibliography.
2. Computer-assisted instruction—United States—Bibliography.
3. Computer-managed instruction—United States—Bibliography.
I. Title. II. Series: Garland bibliographies in contemporary education ; v. 8. III. Series: Garland reference library of social science ; v. 369.
Z5814.A85D5 1988
[LB1028.43]
016.3713'9445—dc19 88-23642
CIP

To my wife, Roberta, and children, Joshua and Sarah, who've helped and supported me in this as well as in all of my academic pursuits.

CONTENTS

INTRODUCTION

The world is in the midst of a revolution every bit as powerful as the Industrial Revolution with which we have been engaged these past 200 years. As the Industrial Revolution extended the physical power of individuals, this new revolution has begun to extend the mental power of individuals. The chief instrument that has fueled the fire in this revolution has been the computer.

During the last decade computer technology has crossed the threshold of the research laboratory and entered the educational environments to lead and promulgate this new mental revolution. Much heralded, the microtechnic revolution has played a role in reshaping, restructuring, and reinvigorating schools in a manner never seen before. The small stand-alone microcomputer has been the chief architect in this process, and, it is hoped, is changing many of the standard instructional interactions that have long been a part of schooling.

The acceptance of the tools of this revolution cannot be dismissed. Current estimates put the sales of microcomputers to schools at well over 500,000. Laws mandating the teaching of and use of computer technology at various educational levles have also been passed in many states and local communities. Computer literacy has taken its place with other forms of literacy as part of our educational lexicon.

Following in the wake of these developments researchers began to look at how the introduction of this new technology and its concurrent explosion in information management and skills might affect students, teachers, parents, school environments, and society as a whole. These investigations have focused on four areas.

First, descriptions of the computer and its effects on human thinking and learning, with applications to various aspects of curriculum and subject matter. These studies include examinations of the sociocultural impact of technology.

Second, studies on the use of computers in teaching situations. These examine the possibilities and practices of using computers in various teaching modes. Included in these are ways in which computers can manage instruction, ways in which the computer can carry out instruction on a one-to-one basis with a student, and ways in which the computer can manage data bases and give learners access to data bases. The studies also examine the effectiveness of the computer as an instructional tool.

Third, investigations of some of the problems arising from the use of computers. These relate to problems dealing with the design of instruction for computer use as well as software design and instructional processes. Included in this area are the social and economic dilemmas that arise from the use of computers, both in society and the schools.

Fourth, examinations of the prospects for the use of computers and computer technology in the near and distant future. Within these a look at how computer technology might change school and the nature of schooling has been discussed.

This bibliography focuses on these four areas of research. Publications with relevant reference information have been included. Some of the studies have been annotated to provide a more complete description of the study cited, but there has been no attempt to evaluate the quality of any of the studies cited.

The primary aim of the bibliography is to present researchers with a listing of both primary and secondary works detailing the role of the computer in contemporary education from 1975 through 1986. The starting date of 1975 was chosen primarily because the first massive use of computers in education began in the late 1960's and studies evaluating computer assisted and computer managed instruction began to appear in the early 1970's. By 1975, computers had begun to be looked upon as a promising educational tool, and researchers began a full-scale assault on the technology's usefulness in school settings.

Structure of the Bibliography

Topics Covered

The bibliography focuses on research examining computers and education. Specifically, it relates studies carried out or centering on computers in preschools, elementary schools, and secondary schools. It contains citations ranging from the effectiveness of computer assisted instruction to studies on aggression and video games.

Because of the diverse nature and range of studies as well as their cross-disciplinary and cross-topical characteristics, a content listing would have garnered more than 100 entries. To simplify locating references, only four major subject areas have been identified. Within these four headings all listings are presented alphabetically, by author. Extensive subject and author indexes are provided to make cross-referencing easier.

The studies covered in this bibliography include short term as well as longitudinal works. Articles, reviews, and dissertations as well as books were reviewed for inclusion in this work. All types of research methodologies are covered.

Topics Not Covered

Several topics relating to computers and schooling have been excluded. A major reason for this was to limit the length of the bibliography. Many of these topics could form the basis for future bibliographies.

Except for a few postings, studies relating to computer literacy have been excluded. Most of the extensive computer literacy studies have been subsumed within broader studies of computer/school applications. Early studies of computer literacy were eliminated because of the chronology of the bibliography.

Studies of computer applications and uses in postsecondary and adult education, with the exception of those that relate their findings to elementary or secondary education have been excluded. Postsecondary uses of computers in educational and training situations have been of a different nature. A bibliography of training applications or adult learning would seem to be a better location for these studies.

Military and commercial use of computers as educational tools has been excluded. The nature of technological use in these settings is for different purposes than in traditional school environments.

Studies conducted outside the United States have been excluded with the exception of several conducted in Canada. A major reason for this is that the results of these studies are not widely available in this country and the findings may not be applicable to school situations in this country.

Conference papers that are not available from the author, the ERIC system, or through conference proceedings have been excluded. While some papers that are important to understanding the use of technology in schools fall into this category, the issue of accessibility precluded their listing.

Sources of References

The major data bases used to locate documents were: *Education Index*, *Dissertation Abstracts*, *Resources in Education*, *Current Index to Journals of Education* (CIJE), and *Educational Resources Information Center* (ERIC). In addition, several document based data systems were used as cross references.

To locate books and texts not listed in the above data bases, a search of *Books in Print* for the years used in the bibliography was also undertaken.

Types of Documents Included

The focus of the bibliography was on research reports, technical reports, details of research studies, data analysis, articles summarizing findings, and compilations of research. Most are written for application and study purposes in nontechnical jargon.

Reviews of research, including meta analysis, technical reports of ongoing or completed studies and statistical reports detailing the status of computer education have been included.

Some documents detailing the same or similar studies as previous or other listings are indicated by either title similarities or notes.

Research on Computers and Education

Although the computer has not been used as an instructional tool for a great length of time, it has been used long enough so that researchers have been able to examine its usefulness and role in instructional situations. In 1980, Robert P. Taylor spoke of the broad uses of computers in schools as tutors, tools, and tutees. Researchers quickly went beyond that beginning definition and began to look at how computers were being used in several scholastic endeavors.

Computers have often been used to help control the academic instructional process by monitoring the basic key factors in the administration of the educational process. More simply, these are system attempts to keep track of all essential data on courses, students, and instruction. The research done in this area has, for example, looked at instructional effectiveness and time on task and mastery learning.

These systems integrate all instructional records into an operational process that functions continuously. Researchers have been able to use these systems to look at how and when learning occurs, reinforcement strategies, and effective feedback techniques.

Another application of computers to education has been the use of the computer to manage the instructional material and the learners' interacting with the instructional system. This application, called computer managed instruction or CMI, is a series of diagnostic and prescriptive processes involving the learner, the instructor, and a computerized delivery system in which the computer assumes a significant role in instructional guidance and administrative assistance. Research done in this area examines the interaction of content and instruction in a time delivery format.

The application of computers to education that is by far the most sophisticated is computer assisted instruction or CAI. CAI is an online interactive process involving the learner and the computer delivery system in which the computer assumes a direct instructional role. Extensive research into the effectiveness of such systems has taken place throughout the past decade. Not only have private researchers delved into this area, but government sponsored studies have consistently looked at CAI in a variety of educational settings.

Yet another application of the computer has been in the developing and managing of large amounts of information. Data base development, storage, and application have all been looked at by researchers in terms of information processing, storage, retrieval, and dissemination.

How information will be managed and who will have access to it are other broad areas of inquiry that researchers have looked at over the past decade. The sociocultural as well as economic implications of computers in school situations have broad implications for educational policy and decision-making not only for now but for future generations. Access to hardware, gender issues, and economic development via computer training are but a few issues discussed in these type inquiries.

Overview of Bibliographic Topics

Preschool

Items listed in this section cover research carried out in preschool settings, kindergarten settings, and some other early childhood school settings. LOGO research, parental involvement, and controlled environmental studies are included in this section.

Elementary Education

Reports in this section detail research that has implications for children in grades 1 through 6. Content studies in reading, language arts, mathematics as well as other subject areas appear in this section. Effectiveness studies, time on task, and status of the technology in elementary school situations are also mentioned.

Secondary Education

Entries in this section relate research on computers and education that have implications for grades 6–12. Studies of content applications, CAI, CMI, as well as video game research appear here.

General

This section includes citations that have implications for all grade levels. These reports cut across grade level boundaries and develop ideas that could be used in many different grades.

Sources of Information

The libraries at The University of Texas at San Antonio, The University of Texas at Austin, and Trinity University in

San Antonio formed the basic book and periodical collections that I used in preparing this bibliography. In addition, searches of over 200 different data bases at The University of Texas at San Antonio, *Dissertations in Print*, and interlibrary loan were also used throughout this project. I would like to thank all the librarians and reference librarians at the above named institutions for their help and assistance. I would especially like to thank Charles Thurston, reference librarian at The University of Texas at San Antonio, for his help throughout this project.

Reference

Taylor, Robert, ed. *The Computer in the School: Tutor, Tool, Tutee.* New York: Teachers College Press, 1980.

Computers in Education

Preschool

1. Atkinson, B. "Learning Disabled Students and LOGO." Journal of Learning Disabilities 8 (1984): 27-45.

   Describes how learning disabled students are using LOGO in a variety of classroom skills. Recommends that LOGO be used in developing thinking skills in LD classrooms.

2. Barnes, B.J., and S. Hill. "Should Young Children Work with Microcomputers - LOGO Before LEGO?" The Computing Teacher 9 (1983): 11-14.

   Presents research on effects of introducing LOGO to preschool age children. Questions effectiveness of early computer interactions.

3. Beeson, B.S., and R.A. Williams. The Effects of Gender and Age on Preschool Children's Choice of the Computer As a Child's Selected Activity. Muncie, IN: Ball State University, 1983.

   Describes differences in activities of young children when computers are introduced in play environments. Relates that there are no differences in terms of gender on child's use of technology.

4. Brown, S.W., and M.K. Rood. "Training Students in LOGO and BASIC: What's the Difference?" Paper presented at the annual meeting of the American Educational Research Association, New Orleans, April 1984.

   Discusses logical thinking structures inherent in LOGO and BASIC and functions of each in training students. Suggests LOGO may be more beneficial as a beginning language.

5. Burbles, N.C., and P. Reese. Teaching Logic To Children: An Exploratory Study of "Rocky's Boots." Berkeley: University of California, 1984.

Reviews logic applications of "Rocky's Boots" as a means of teaching critical thinking skills. Notes that this is an exemplary program in this area.

6. Burg, K. "The Microcomputer in the Kindergarten." Young Children 3 (1984): 28-33.

Presents current applications and trends of computer use in kindergarten settings. Applications are focused in recognition and recall programs with some use of LOGO for critical thinking development.

7. Burns, G., M. Cook, and B. Dubitisky. "The LOGO Project at Bank Street: A Perspective on Children, Teachers, and Computers." Paper presented at the National Educational Computing Conference, Kansas City, June 1982.

Describes how teachers and children use LOGO as part of everyday school life and how computers alter teacher/student interactions.

8. BYTE. August 1985.

Special issue on LOGO, its uses and applications with young children in school settings.

9. Clements, D.H. Computers in Early and Primary Education. Englewood Cliffs, NJ: Prentice Hall, 1985.

Compendium of current views and practices of computer usage in preschool, early, and primary grades. Offers some suggestions for more effective applications of computer technology. Author is an advocate of computers in early education.

10. ______. "Effects of LOGO Programming on Cognition, Metacognitive Skills, and Achievement." Paper presented at the annual meeting of the American Educational Research Association, Chicago, April 1985.

Describes how the development of LOGO programming skill effects a broad range of cognitive skill development and achievement. Suggests there may be carry over effect in other subject matter.

11. _____. "Longitudinal Study of the Effects of LOGO Programming on Achievement and Cognitive Abilities." Paper presented at the annual meeting of the American Educational Research Association, Chicago, April 1985.

Discusses the effects of LOGO in terms of long term effectiveness in developing thinking and logic skills.

12. _____, and D.F. Gullo. "Effects of Computer Programming on Young Children's Cognition." Journal of Educational Psychology 76 (1984): 1051-1058.

Relates how young children's reasoning power and cognitive development may be positively effected by exposure to programming skills.

13. Cuffaro, H.K. "Microcomputers in Education: Why Is Earlier Better?" Teacher's College Record 85 (1984): 559-568.

Relates that microcomputers may not be a desirable learning tool for young children because learning styles of preschool children are not often compatible with computer-assisted learning techniques.

14. Cunningham, S. "Off To a Good Start with Microcomputers." Educational Computer 1 (1981): 38-39.

Discusses microcomputers in early education settings.

15. Fire Dog, P. "Exciting Effects of LOGO in an Urban Public School System." Educational Leadership 43 (1985): 45-47.

Describes the introduction to LOGO in an urban school and its positive effects in making children aware of technology.

16. Flank, S. "Little Hands on the Computer." G/C/T 25 (1982): 28-29.

Describes computer usage with young (preschool and kindergarten) children who have been identified as gifted and talented. Instructional sequences mentioned include development of programming and computer literacy skills.

17. Galanter, E. Kids and Computers. New York: Putnam, 1983.

Overview of the effects that computer technology has had on everyday and school life of young children.

18. Globerson, T. "Stylistic Differences In Learning LOGO." Paper presented at the LOGO '85 Conference, Cambridge, June 1985.

Discusses how learning styles may affect the ways in which LOGO is learned and applied.

19. Goldstein, I. The Computer As Coach: An Athletic Paradigm for Intellectual Education (LOGO Memo 37). Cambridge, MA: MIT Artificial Intelligence Laboratory, 1976.

Reviews ways that computer technology can be used to coach and prepare students for a variety of learning experiences.

20. Grabe, M., and C. Grabe. "The Microcomputer and the Language Experience Approach." Reading Teacher 38 (1985): 508-511.

Describes how computers can be used as part of the language experience reading program in building content and cognitive skills through use of word processing programs.

21. Grant, J., and P. Semmes. "A Rationale for LOGO for Hearing-Impaired Preschoolers." American Annals of the Deaf 128 (1983): 564-569.

Discusses how LOGO can be used in an interactive learning environment with hearing-impaired young children.

22. Hawkins, J. "Learning LOGO Together: The Social Context." Paper presented at the annual meeting of the American Educational Research Association, Montreal, April 1983.

23. ______. The Interpretation of LOGO in Practice (Technical Report). New York: Bank Street College, Center For Children and Technology, 1984.

24. Hines, S. "Computer Programming Abilities of Five-Year-Old Children." Educational Computer (July/August 1983): 10-12.

Description of beginning programming for preschool and early elementary aged children.

25. Howe, J. "LOGO Programming and Intermediate Mathematics." Computers in Education (March 1985): 7-10.

Relates how LOGO can be used to teach mathematics in intermediate grades.

26. Huntgate, H., and J.I. Heller. "Preschool Children and Microcomputers." Paper presented at the annual meeting of the American Educational Research Association, New Orleans, April 1984.

27. Jewson, J., and R.D. Pea. "LOGO Research at Bank Street College." BYTE (1982): 332-333.

Overview of first large-scale research projects involving LOGO at selected school sites and in a variety of age groups ranging from preschool to upper elementary.

28. Johnson, J.E. "Characteristics of Pre-Schoolers Interested in Microcomputers." Journal of Educational Research 78 (1985): 299-305.

Describes types of children interested in working with computers and their home, school, and parental interests. Findings indicate that parental and environmental factors are strongest in gaining child's technological interest in computers.

29. Klinzing, D.G. "A Study of the Behavior of Children In a Preschool Equipped with Computers." Paper presented at the annual meeting of the American Educational Research Association, Chicago, April 1985.

30. Kulik, J.A. "Evaluating the Effects of Teaching with Computers." Microcomputers in Early Education. Edited by P. Campbell and J. Fein. Reston, VA: Keston Publishing Co., 1984.

Describes long-term studies of computers in early years along with effects of critical thinking and analysis.

31. Lipinski, J.M. Competence, Gender and Preschooler's Free Play Choices When a Microcomputer Is Present in the Classroom. Greensboro, NC: North Carolina Family Research Center, 1984.

Presents reaction of children in a play environment towards computers. Also discusses how and when they choose computers as a play device.

32. Lough, T. "WATERCROSS: A LOGO Exploration." Computing Teacher 10 (1982): 51-54.

Description and use of a LOGO program.

33. Lutz, J.E., and P.A. Taylor. "A Computerized Home-Based Curriculum for High-Risk Preschoolers." AEDS Journal 15 (1981): 1-9.

Description of CAI curriculum for economically disadvantaged preschool children who have been identified as having learning problems.

34. Maddux, C.D. "The Educational Promise of LOGO." Computers in the Schools 1 (1984): 79-89.

Overview of ways LOGO is being used in schools in a variety of settings.

35. Margot, C., and N. Armstrong. "Computers For The Preschool: Beyond the Basics." ERIC ED 250 057, 1984.

36. Meringoff, L. "Influence of the Medium on Children's Story Apprehension." Journal of Educational Psychology 72 (1980): 240-249.

37. Muller, A.A., and M. Perlmutter. "Preschool Children's Problem Solving Interactions at Computers and Jigsaw Puzzles." ERIC ED 248 013, 1984.

38. Nida, R.E. Introducing a Microcomputer to a Preschool Classroom: The Effects on Children's Social Interaction. Greensboro, NJ: North Carolina Family Research Center, 1984.

Relates both positive and negative socialization effects of computers in a preschool program in terms of overall social interaction processes.

39. Olson, D., and N. Torrance. "Literacy and Cognitive Development: A Conceptual Transformation in the Early School Years." Issues in Childhood Cognitive Development. Edited by S. Meadows. London: Methuen, 1983.

Relates use of computer technology and cognitive development of children.

40. Papert, S. "Computer Criticism vs. Technocentric Thinking." LOGO '85 Theoretical Papers 1 (1985): 53-58.

Discusses LOGO critics and need for developing thinking skills with computer competency.

41. ______. Mindstorms: Children, Computers and Powerful Ideas. New York: Basic Books, 1980.

Classic work on LOGO, its philosophy, and the relationship of critical thinking and problem solving with the development of the LOGO language.

42. ______, D. Watt, A. DiSessa, and S. Weir. "Final Report of the Brookline LOGO Project, Part III: Project Summary and Data Analysis (LOGO Memo No. 53)." ERIC ED 196 423, 1979.

43. Pea, R.D. LOGO Programming and Problem Solving (Technical Report No. 12). New York: Bank Street College of Education, Center for Technology and Children, 1983.

Discusses use of LOGO programming skills as a centerpiece in developing problem-solving skills.

44. ______. "LOGO Programming and Problem Solving." Symposium conducted at the annual meeting of the American Educational Research Association, Montreal, April 1983.

45. ______. "Symbol Systems and Thinking Skills: LOGO in Context." Proceedings of the 1984 LOGO Conference. Cambridge, MA: Massachusetts Institute of Technology, 1984.

46. ______, and J. Hawkins. "Children's Planning Processes in a Chore-Scheduling Task." Blueprints for Thinking: The Role of Planning in Cognitive Development. Edited by S.L. Friedmont, E.K. Scholnick, and R.R. Cocking. New York: Cambridge University Press, 1984.

Discusses development of planning skills as used in computer programming as a device for cognitive skill development.

47. ______, J. Hawkins, and K. Sheingold. "Developmental Studies on Learning in LOGO Computer Programming." Abstracts from the Society for Research in Child Development, Washington, 1983.

48. ______, and D.M. Kurland. LOGO Programming and the Development of Planning Skills. (Technical Report No. 16). New York: Bank Street College of Education, Center for Children and Technology, 1984.

Discusses how thinking skills that are developed in LOGO interactions assist in the use of planning and critical thinking skills.

49. ______, and D.M. Kurland. "On the Cognitive Effects of Learning Computer Programming." New Ideas in Psychology 2 (1984): 137-168.

Ways in which concepts developed in programming skills can be transferred to other areas of thinkning/skill development.

50. ______, D.M. Kurland, and J. Hawkins. "LOGO and the Development of Thinking Skills." Children and Microcomputers: Research on the Newest Medium. Edited by M. Chen and W. Paisley. Beverly Hills, CA: Sage, 1985.

Essay on the development of critical thinking techniques within a LOGO environment.

51. Perlman, R. Using Computer Technology to Provide a Creative Learning Environment for Preschool Children (LOGO Memo No. 24). Cambridge, MA: MIT Artificial Intelligence Laboratory, 1976.

52. Piel, J.A., and W.A. Baller. "Effect of Computer Assistance on Acquisition of Piagetian Conceptualization Among Children of Ages Two to Four." AEDS Journal 19 (1986): 210-215.

Age and computer exposure found to increase ability to acquire Piagetian concepts.

53. Piestrup, A.M. "Young Children Use Apple II To Test Reading Skills Program." ERIC ED 202 476, 1981.

54. ______. "Early Learning of Logic and Geometry Using Microcomputers. Final Report." ERIC ED 202 477, 1982.

55. ______. "Young Children Use Computer Graphics." ERIC ED 224 564, 1982.

56. Rieber, L.P. "The Effect of LOGO on Young Children." Paper presented at the annual convention of the Association for Educational Communications and Technology, Las Vegas, 1986.

57. Rothenberg, D. "Research on Young Children's Keyboarding." Micronotes on Children and Computers 1 (1984): 1-4.

58. Rubin, K.H., and C. Seibel. "The Effects of Ecological Setting on the Cognitive and Social Play Behaviors of Preschoolers." Paper presented at the annual meeting of the American Educational Research Association, San Francisco, April 1979.

59. Seidman, R. "The Effects of Learning Computer Programming Language on the Logical Reasoning of School Children." Paper presented at the annual meeting of the American Educational Association, Los Angeles, April 1981.

60. Shade, D.D. Microcomputers: A Close Look ast What Happens When Preschool Children Interact with Age Appropriate Software. Greensboro, NC: North Carolina Family Research Center, 1983.

Presents studies on the effects of different software. Visual stimulus and cognitive levels appear to be important factors in program effectiveness.

61. Silvern, S.D., P.A. Williamson, and T.A. Countermine. "Aggression in Young Children and Video Game Play." Paper presented at the biennal meeting of the Society for Research in Child Development, Detroit, April 1983.

62. ______, P.A. Williamson, and T.A. Countermine. "Children's Play with Video Games." Paper presented at the International Conference on Play and Play Environments, Austin, June 1983.

63. Simon, T. "Play and Learning with Computers." Early Childhood Development and Care (19): 69-78.

Discussion of use of computers with preschoolers in play/choice situations. Relates ways children use computers during interactive play sequences.

64. Smithy-Willis, D. "Visual Discrimination and Preschoolers." Educational Computer (2): 19, 45.

Presents use of computers to determine visual differences

65. Solomon, C., and S. Papert. A Case Study of a Young Child Doing Turtle Graphics in LOGO (Artificial Intelligence Laboratory Memo 375). Cambridge, MA: MIT Artificial Intelligence Laboratory, 1976.

First studies of LOGO and use of graphics with young children.

66. Sprigle, J.E., and L. Schaefer. "Age, Gender and Spatial Knowledge Influences on Preschoolers' Computer Programming Ability." Early Child Development and Care (14): 243-250.

Development of programming ability is tied to an understanding of spatial relationships in this study.

67. Stein, J.S., and M.C. Linn. Cognitive Consequences of Software Design Features: An Investigation of "Rocky's Boots." Berkeley: University of California, 1984.

Analyzes software design and its effects on the development of logical thinking skills.

68. ______, and M.C. Linn. Research Designs for Studies of Acquisition of Higher Cognitive Skills from Computer-Assisted Learning. Substudy B2: "Rocky's Boots." Berkeley: University of California, 1984.

69. Strand, E. "A Descriptive Study Comparing Preschool and Kindergarten LOGO Interaction." Paper presented at the annual meeting of the American Educational Research Association, San Francisco, 1986.

70. Strien, W., and W. Kachman. "Effects of Computer Games on Young Children's Co-Operative Behavior: An Exploratory Study." Journal of Research and Development in Education (18): 40-43.

Discussion of competitive nature of children versus cooperative behavior while using a computer game. Indications are that children will cooperate in solving computer generated problem sequences.

71. Swigger, K., and J. Campbell. "The Computer Goes to Nursery School." Educational Computer (1): 10-12.

Overview of types of uses of computers in nursery school settings.

72. Swigger, K.M., and B.K. Swigger. "Social Patterns and Computer Use Among Preschool Children." AEDS Journal (17): 35-41.

Gender, age, and computer use in preschool settings.

73. Tan, L.E. "Computers in Preschool Education." Early Childhood Development and Care (19): 319-336.

Present cognitive and developmental consequences, both positive and negative, of introducing computers to preschoolers.

74. Tessmer, K.M. "Children Using Computers: What Are They Doing? What Are They Really Learning?" ERIC ED 252 192, 1984.

75. Thompson, B., and T. Cloer. " A Learning Aid: Imaginative Electronics Applied to Education." Young Children in a Computerized Environment. Edited by M. Frank. New York: Haworth Press, 1982.

Applications of computer uses for young children.

76. Vartuli, S. "Research on Using Computers with Preschool Age Children." ERIC ED 256 516, 1984.

Compendium of current research on computers in a preschool environment.

77. Watt, D.H. "A Comparison of The Problem Solving Styles of Two Students Learning LOGO: A Computer Language for Children." Creative Computing (5): 86-90.

Discusses studies of field dependent and independent learning styles in conjunction with computer use discussed.

78. Watt, D.H. "The Brookline LOGO Project. Final Report Part III. Profiles of Individual Students' Work. AI Memo No. 546." ERIC ED 196 424, 1979.

79. ______. "LOGO in the Schools." BYTE 116-134.

Update on LOGO applications in school settings.

80. Weir, S. Using LOGO to Cataliyze Communication in an Autistic Child (Research Report No. 15). Edinburgh: University of Edinburgh, Department of Artificial Intelligence, 1976.

81. ______. LOGO As An Information Prosthetic for the Handicapped (Working Paper No. 9). Cambridge, MA: MIT Artificial Intelligence Laboratory, 1981.

82. ______. Weir, S. "LOGO and the Exceptional Child." Microcomputing (September 1981): 78-84.

83. Worden, P.E. "Preschoolers' Alphabet Learning Activities with Their Parents: Picture Books Versus Personal Computer Software." Paper presented at the biennial meeting of the Society For Research In Child Development, Toronto, April 1985.

84. Zelman, S. "Individual Differences and the Computer Learning Environment: Motivational Constraints to Learning LOGO." Paper presented at the annual meeting of the American Educational Research Association, Chicago, April 1985.

Elementary Education

85. Abram, S.L. "The Effect of Computer Assisted Instruction on Grade Phonics and Mathematics Achievement Computation." Ph.D. dissertation. Northern Arizona University, 1984.

86. Alderman, D.L., S.S. Swinton, and J.S. Braswell. "Assessing Basic Arithmetic Skills and Understanding Across Curricula: Computer-Assisted Instruction and Compensatory Education." Journal of Children's Mathematical Behavior (2): 3-28.

    Results of research in Title I schools using computers to teach remedial subjects. Notes that groups using computers increased basic skill development at a faster rate than those involved in traditional instruction.

87. Anand, P.G. "Using Computer-Assisted Instruction to Personalize Arithmetic Materials for Elementary School Children." Ph.D. dissertation. Memphis State University, 1985.

88. Andolina, M. "Reading Tests: Traditioinal Vs. Computerized. Which Will Benefit Student--and Teacher?" Classroom Computer News (2): 39-40.

    Discusses use of computer to evaluate reading skills in elementary schools.

89. Archambeault, B.J.C. "The Relationship Between Interaction Time and Reading Math Achievement for Chapter I Students Using Computer-Assisted Instruction in Grades Three, Four and Five." Ph.D. dissertation. Louisiana State University and Agricultural and Mechanical College, 1986.

90. Atkins, V.F. "A Comparison of the Effect of Experimenter and Microcomputer Delivered Knowledge of Results on the Response Speed of Nonretarded and Mentally Retarded Students." Ph.D. dissertation. Oregon State University, 1984.

91. Attisha, M., and M. Yazdani. "An Expert System for Diagnosing Children's Multiplication Scores." Instructional Science 13 (1984): 79-92.

Presents expert program for score diagnosis.

92. Babcock, N.L. "Computers in Special Education: A Practical Approach to New Technology." Spectrum 2 (1984): 19-21.

Evaluates ways to use computers for all ranges of special education children.

93. Baker, P.C. "A Comparison of Live, Videotaped, and Interactive Computer-Assisted Instructional Methodologies in the Teaching of Bliss Symbols to Institutionalized Mentally Retarded Persons." Ph.D. dissertation. University of Mississippi, 1985.

94. Balajthy, E. "Artificial Intelligence and the Teaching of Reading and Writing by Computers." Journal of Reading 29 (1985): 23-32.

AI program development is reviewed as well as possible ways to use it in reading and writing skill development. Call for a further development in this area and an increased integration of AI programs and computer software in reading.

95. Ballinger, W.L. "The Design of a Computer Assisted Instruction System for the Visually Handicapped." Ph.D. dissertation. North Carolina State University, 1978.

96. Barclay, J.A. "A Comparison of Programmed Instruction and Game Strategies for Teaching Selected Map Concepts to Children Through Computer Assisted Instruction." Ph.D. dissertation. Auburn University, 1985.

97. Barr, A., M. Beard, and R.C. Atkinson. *The Computer As A Tutorial Laboratory: The Stanford BIP Project* (Technical Report 260). Stanford, CA: Stanford University Institute for Mathematical Studies in the Social Sciences, 1975.

Effectiveness of computer as a tutor in mathematics.

98. Bass, G. "Teaching Basic Skills through Microcomputer Assisted Instruction." *Journal of Educational Computing Research* 2 (1986): 207-219.

Study using microcomputers to assess effectiveness of CAI showed only one experimental groups statistically significant in reading and math scores and no attitudinal differences related towards school or sense of control.

99. Battista, M.T., and G.H. Krockover. "The Effects of Computer Use in Science and Mathematics Education upon the Computer Literacy of Preservice Elementary Teachers." *Journal of Research in Science Teaching* 21 (1984): 39-46.

Computers used to upgrade computer literacy skills in college setting considered successful. Computer literacy skills developed in integrated learning setting considered a positive attribute of this study.

100. _____, and K.J. Steele. "The Effect of Computer-Assisted and Computer Programming Instruction on the Computer Literacy of High Ability Fifth Grade Students." *School Science and Mathematics* 84 (1984): 649-658.

Research study on the effects of CAI in teaching computer literacy and programming skills. Results indicate positive responses to CAI.

101. Beasley, W.A. "Microcomputer Applications in the Education of the Gifted." Ph.D. dissertation. University of Georgia, 1985.

102. Becnel, S.T. "CABS Project, Computers and Basic Skills: A Design Model for Writing Computer Programs That Teach Basic Skills to LD and SL Students." Paper presented at the International Convention of the

Association for Children with Learning Disabilities, San Francisco, CA: February 1985.

103. Berg, R. "Resisting Change: What the Literature Says About Computers in the Social Studies Classroom." *Social Education* 47 (1983): 314-316.

Use of technology in social studies classes follows resistance patterns typical of many environmental interventions as discussed in research literature related to school change patterns.

104. Bigum, C., and A. Gilding. "A Video Monitoring Technique for Investigating Computer-Based Learning Programs." *Computers and Education* 9 (1985): 95-99.

Discusses use of video time stop program to measure learning development.

105. Bitter, G.G. "Microcomputers Go to School." *Interface* 8 (1981): 2-9.

Examines ways that microcomputers are being used in school classrooms and by administrators.

106. Blakeway, E.G. "Drill, Practice and Testing Applications for the Reluctant Learner and Teacher of Mathematics: Elementary and Secondary." Paper presented at the annual conference of the National Association of Users Of Computer Applications To Learning, Portland, October 1976.

107. Blanchard, J.S. "Computer-Assisted Instruction in Today's Reading Classrooms." *Journal of Reading* 23 (1980): 430-434.

Overview of computer uses in reading classrooms such as comprehension skill development, word and sentence placement in text and grammar/language skill development.

108. ______, and D.S. Daniel. "Editorial Comment: Guest Commentary. The Second Coming of Computers in Reading: Hope or Hysteria?" *Reading Psychology* 4 (1983): 3-7.

109. Blaschke, C.L. "Microcomputers in Special Education: Trends and Projections." *Journal Of Special Education Technology* 5 (1982): 25-27.

Reviews ways computer technology is being used to assist physically and learning disabled students.

110. Blum, I., and M. Furlong. "The Writing to Read Project." Momentum 14 (1983): 4-6.

Discusses computers and word processing programs in the teaching of writing.

111. Bolter, J.D. "Computers for Composing." Chameleon In The Classroom: Developing Roles for Computers (Technical Report No. 22). Edited by R. Case. New York: Bank Street College of Education, 1983.

Analyzes writing skill development and the use of computers and word processing programs.

112. Bork, A. "Children and Interactive Learning Environments." Children and Microcomputers: Research on the Newest Medium. Edited by M. Chen and W. Paisley. Beverly Hills, CA: Sage, 1985.

Presents discussion of interactive nature of computer learning environments.

113. Bradley, V.N. "Improving Students' Writing with Microcomputers." Language Arts 59 (1982): 732-738.

Discusses use of computers and word processing programs in children's writing.

114. Brangret-Drowns, R.L. "Effectiveness of Computer Based Education in Secondary Schools." Journal of Computer-Based Instruction 12 (1985): 59-68.

Discusses comparative study of computer-based education with traditional learning. Focus is on areas that have made most use of computers (mathematics, English composition, and science). Results mixed with most effective areas being in mathematics.

115. Brawley, G.L. "Effects of Types of Reinforcers and an Achievement Motivator Interacting with Aptitude on Latency Rate in Computer Assisted Mathematics Instruction." Ph.D. dissertation. University of San Francisco, 1984.

116. Brooks, D.B. "A Survey of Youth Between Ten and Eighteen Years of Age Who Frequent Video Arcades and Other Locations with Video Games." Video Games and Human Development: Research Agenda for the '80s. Cambridge, MA: Harvard University Graduate School Of Education, 1983.

117. Brown, B. "PLATO Promises Grade Gains." Electronic Education 2 (1981): 10-12.

Use of PLATO in elementary school settings.

118. Brown, J.S. "Process Versus Product: A Perspective on Tools for Communal and Informal Electronic Learning." Children and Microcomputers: Research on the Newest Medium. Edited by M. Chen and W. Paisley. Beverly Hills, CA: Sage, 1985.

119. Brunken, P. "Independence for the Visually Handicapped Through Technology." Paper presented at the annual convention of the Council for Exceptional Children, Washington, April 1984.

120. Bryg, V. "The Effect of Computer Assisted Instruction upon Reading Achievement with Selected Fourth Grade Children." Ph.D. dissertation. University of Pennsylvania, 1984.

121. Bukatman, K.L. "The Effects of Computer Assisted Instruction for Mastery of Multiplication Facts on Learning Disabled Elementary School Aged Children Differing on Locus of Control." Ph.D. dissertation. Boston College, 1981.

122. Bumgarner, K.M. "Effects of Informational Feedback and Social Reinforcement on Elementary Students' Achievement During CAI Drill and Practice on Multiplication Facts." Ph.D. dissertation. Seattle University, 1984.

123. Burns, P.K. "A Quantitative Synthesis of Research Findings Relative to the Pedagogical Effectiveness of Computer Assisted Mathematics Instruction in Elementary and Secondary Schools." Ph.D. dissertation. University of Iowa, 1981.

124. Bychowski, D.K., and R. Van Dusseldrop. "Computer Literacy and Use Among Elementary Classroom Teachers." ERIC ED 249 938, 1984.

125. Caldwell, R.M. "Computers and Computer Courseware: New Directions for Helping Children Learn." _Journal of Children in Contemporary Society_ 14 (1981): 55-71.

Discusses effective program designs that encourage higher cognitive learning. Programs that involve problem solving are rated most effective.

126. Cannara, A.B. "Experiments in Teaching Children Computer Programming." Technical Report No. 271. ERIC ED 135 327, 1976.

127. Carey, D.M. "An Investigation Of Factors That Affect Elementary School Teachers' Educational Use Of Computers." Ph.D. dissertation. University of Oregon, 1985.

128. Carman, G.O., and B. Kosberg. "Educational Technology Research: Computer Technology and the Education of Emotionally Handicapped Children." _Educational Technology_ 2 (1982): 26-30.

Discussion of computers with EH children and behavior modification techniques.

129. Carrier, C. "Selection of Options by Field Independent and Dependent Children in Computer Based Concept Lessons." _Journal of Computer-Based Instruction_ 11 (1984): 49-54.

130. ______. "Using Micrcomputers with Fourth Grade Students To Reinforce Arithmetic Skills." _Journal of Computer-Based Instruction_ 16 (1985): 45-51.

Evaluates remedial and reinforcement techniques.

131. Cartwright, G.F., and J.L. Derevensky. "An Attitudinal Study of Computer-Assisted Testing As a Learning Method." _Psychology in the Schools_ 13 (1976): 317-321.

Students and teachers both questioned as to their feelings on using and interacting with computers.

132. Carver, R.P., and J.V. Hoffman. "The Effect of Practice Through Repeated Reading on Gain in Reading Ability Through Using a Computer Instructional System." Reading Research Quarterly 16 (1981): 374-390.

Computer was used as tool to teach and measure increased reading capacity.

133. Chaing, A. Demonstration Of Computer-Assisted Instruction with Handicapped Children. Arlington, VA: RMC Research Corporation, 1978.

134. Chamberlin, E. "Language Development Component, Compensatory Language Experiences and Reading Program. Final Evaluation Report." ERIC ED 249 247, 1983.

135. Char, C.A. Research and Design Issues Concerning Development of Educational Software For Children. New York: Bank Street College of Education Center for Children and Technology, 1983.

136. Chen, M. "Computers in the Lives of Our Children: Looking Back on a Generation Of Television Research." The New Media: Communication, Research and Technology. Edited by R.E. Rice. Beverly Hills, CA: Sage, 1984.

Compares research on television with studies on effectiveness of the computer as a learning tool.

137. ______. "A Macro-Focus on Microcomputers: Eight Utilization and Effects Issues." Children and Microcomputers: Research on the Newest Medium. Edited by M. Chen and W. Paisley. Beverly, CA: Sage, 1985.

138. ______, D. Lieberman, and W. Paisley. "Microworlds of Research." Children and Microcomputers: Research on the Newest Medium. Beverly Hills, CA: Sage, 1985.

Analyzes school environments that use microcomputer technology in terms of research possibilities.

139. ______, and W. Paisley, eds. Children and Microcomputers: Research on the Newest Medium. Beverly Hills, CA: Sage, 1985.

Chapters on various aspects of computer uses and effectiveness in school settings.

140. Churchill, L.D. "The Effectiveness of Sequencing of Computer-Related Training on Elementary Teachers' Attitudes Towards Mathematics, Mathematics Instruction and Computers In Education." Ph.D. dissertation. University of Washington, 1985.

141. Clayborne, B.M. "Dimensions and Correlates of the Attitudes of Inner City Parents Toward Microcomputers in Education." Ph.D. dissertation. University of Maryland, 1985.

142. Collins, A. "Learning to Read and Write with Personal Computers." ERIC ED 229 728, 1983.

143. ______, B.C. Bruce, and A. Rubin. "Microcomputer-Based Writing Activities for the Upper Congress and Exposition of The Society for Applied Learning Technology, Orlando, FL, February, 1982.

144. Cooperman, K.S. "An Experimental Study To Compare The Effectiveness of a Regular Classroom Reading Program to a Regular Classroom Reading Program with Computer Assisted Instruction Program in Reading Comprehension Skills Grades Two Through Four." Ph.D. dissertation. The American University, 1985.

145. Costanzo, W. "Language, Thinking, and the Culture of Computers." <u>Language Arts</u> 62 (1985): 16-23.

Discusses computers as part of the cultural milieu of the classroom.

146. Cox, D., and C.F. Berger. "Microcomputers Are Motivating." <u>Science and Children</u> 19 (1981): 28-29.

Discusses motivational techniques, using microcomputers, in science classrooms.

147. Cranford, H.R. "A Study of the Effects of Computer-Assisted Instruction in Mathematics on the Achievement and Attitude of Pupils in Grades Five and Six in a Rural Setting." Ph.D. dissertation. University of Southern Mississippi, 1976.

148. Darling, D.L. "A Study of the Effects Using Microcomputers on Achievement in Mathematics Basic Skills." Ph.D. dissertation. University of Tennessee, 1986.

149. Davidson, M.S. "Computer Assisted Instruction in Arithmetic for Specific Learning Disabilities in the Elementary School." Ph.D. dissertation. University of South Florida, 1984.

150. Davis, J.E., and J.D. Haas. "Microcomputers in the Social Studies." Paper presented at the annual meeting of the Social Science Consortium, Athens, GA, June 1983.

Uses of computers in social science classrooms and their effectiveness as a learning tool.

151. Dembowski, F.L. "The Effects of Declining Enrollments on The Instructional Programs of Public Elementary and Secondary Schools." Paper presented at the annual meeting of the American Educational Research Association, Boston, April 1980.

152. Dickinson, W.P., and M.A. Vereen. "Two Students at One Microcomputer." _Theory into Practice_ 22 (1983): 296-300.

Discussion on how many students can use a computer and still maintain it as an effective classroom tool.

153. Diem, R.A. "Preparation for the Technological Classroom: Can We Fulfill The Need?" Paper presented at the annual meeting of the Social Studies Education Consortium, Athens, GA, June 1983.

Teacher education needs to include computer literacy as part of its goals if it is to prepare effective and future oriented teachers.

154. Doerr, C. _Microcomputers and the 3 R's: A Guide for Teachers_. Rochelle Park, NJ: Hayden Publishing Co., 1979.

Applications for computers at various elementary levels.

155. Dreyer, L.G., K.R. Futtersak, and A.E. Boehm. "Sight Words for the Computer Age: An Essential Word List." _The Reading Teacher_ 39 (1985): 12-15.

156. Dugdale, S., and D. Kibbey. Fractions Curriculum of The PLATO Elementary School Mathematics Project. Urbana, IL: Computer Based Education Technical Report, University of Illinois, 1975.

Analysis of PLATO fraction curriculum. Includes data on who used the curriculum, time on task, and reaction to problem modes.

157. Dunn, J., and K. Mitchell. "Sample Competency Based Modularized Instructional Systems and Systems Components." ERIC ED 204 624, 1981.

158. Durnin, R.G. "Computer Based Education: A Study of Student Interactions and Achievement In Small Group and Individual Settings." Ph.D. dissertation. Claremont Graduate School, 1985.

159. Easterling, B.A. "The Effects of Computer Assisted Instruction As a Supplement to Classroom Instruction in Reading Comprehension and Arithmetic." Ph.D. dissertation. North Texas State University, 1982.

160. Education Service Center, Region 4, Houston, TX. Developing Basic Skill Proficiencies for Limited English Proficient (LEP) and English As a Second Language (ESL) Students in Vocational Training. ERIC ED 259 106, 1984.

Describes successful use of computers in LEP and ESL vocational training and basic skills programs.

161. Education Turnkey Systems, Inc. "Microcomputers In Special Education." ERIC ED 231 175, 1983.

162. Ehly, S.W., and S.C. Larsen. Peer Tutoring for Individualized Instruction. Boston: Allyn & Bacon, 1980.

Presents use of computers in individualized and peer tutoring sessions for elementary and high school students who have had difficulty in traditional classroom settings.

163. Ekey, D. "Computer Assisted Instruction in Compensatory Education and Chapter 1: A Fact or Fad?" AEDS Monitor 24 (1985): 11-12.

Overview of compensatory education projects using microcomputers to teach remedial and basic skills.

164. Elliot, B.A. "An Investigation of the Effects of Computer Feedback and Interspersed Questions on the Text Comprehension of Poor Readers." Ph.D. dissertation. Temple University, 1986.

165. English, J.P. "Microcomputer Admdinistered Spelling Tests: Effects on Learning Handicapped and Normally Achieving Students." Journal of Reading, Writing and Learning Disabilities International 1 (985): 165-176.

Research study whose results indicate that computer administered tests have a positive effect for both subject groups under study.

166. Evans, P., and M. Rouse. "The Evaluation of a Software Package Giving Practice in Arithmetic for Children with Mild Learning Disabilities." Studies in Educational Evaluation 11 (1985): 55-62.

167. Ewing, R.P. "Computer-Assisted Chapter 1 Instruction." Ph.D. dissertation. Virginia Polytechnic Institute and State University, 1984.

168. Federico, P.A. "Individual Differences in Cognitive Characteristics and Computer Managed Mastery Learning." Journal of Computer-Based Instruction 9 (1982): 10-18.

Study of learning styles and cognitive ability in computer/mastery learning environment. Findings relate that some students have difficulty in a computer learning environment, particularly those who dislike structured learning sequences.

169. Feldman, R., L. Devin-Sheehan, and V. Allen. "Children Tutoring Children: A Critical Review of Research." Children as Teachers: Theory and Research on Tutoring. Edited by V. Allen. New York: Academic Press, 1976.

Overview of research on tutorial programs with critical commentary on children using computers in tutorial environments.

170. Fennell, J.P. "Projection of the Future of Instructional Computing in the Montgomery County Public Schools." ERIC ED 175 459, 1977.

171. Fetler, M. "Sex Differences on the California Statewide Assessment of Computer Literacy." Sex Roles 13 (1985): 181-191.

Findings on computer usage by sex in California schools. Results indicate male students ahead of females in computer literacy.

172. Fey, T.F. "A Comparison of Computer and Teacher Prepared Individualized Reading Prescriptions." Ph.D. dissertation. University of Florida, 1975.

173. Fickel, M.G. "The Effects of LOGO Study on Problem Solving Cognitive Abilities of Sixth Grade Students." Ph.D. dissertation. University of Nebraska-Lincoln, 1986.

174. Fitch, J.L. "Computer-Managed Screening for Communication Disorders." Language, Speech and Hearing Services in the Schools 15 (1984): 66-69.

Methods of using computers in diagnosing and screening children for speech disorders.

175. Fletcher, J.D. "Stanford Project for CAI for Hearing Impaired Students." Journal of Computer Based Instruction (1976): 1-12.

Overview of CAI project that enabled hearing impaired students to use computers as part of instructional activities. Indications are positive for further use in these settings.

176. Forsyth, A.S., Jr. "Applications of Microcomputer Research-Type Adventure Games in Research on Spatial Orientation, Place Location and Memory for Places." Paper presented at the annual meeting of the American Educational Research Association, San Francisco, 1986.

177. Foster, K. "The Influence of Computer-Assisted Instruction and Workbook on the Learning of Multiplication Facts by Learning Disabled and Normal Students."

Ph.D. dissertation. The Florida State University, 1983.

178. Franco, S.M. "How To Design a CAI Course for Mexican American Migrant Students." ERIC ED 212 145, 1981.

179. Frankel, F. "Individualizing Schedules of Instruction for School Children with Learning and Behavioral Problems." Psychology in the Schools 16 (1979): 270-279.

Use of computer to set up individual instructional sequences for children with learning and behavioral disabilities.

180. Frederiksen, J.R. "A Componential Approach to Training Reading Skills." ERIC ED 229 727, 1983.

181. Fricke, J.E. "CAI in a School for the Deaf: Expected Results and a Serendipity or Two." Paper presented at the Association for the Development Of Computer Based Instructional Systems Summer Conference, Minneapolis, August 1976.

182. Friedman, S.G., and A.M. Hofmeister. "Matching Technology to Content and Learners: A Case Study." Exceptional Children 51 (1984): 130-134.

Use of computer technology in setting up individual learning programs for exceptional children.

183. Fulton, R.T. "The Use of Microcomputer Technology in Assessing and Training Communication Skills of Young Hearing Impaired Children." American Annals of the Deaf 128 (1983): 570-576.

Presents and analyzes management and assessment programs for the hearing impaired using a microcomputer.

184. Gadezella, B.M. "A CAI Study Skills Program." ERIC ED 211 059, 1981.

185. Gallion, L.M., and C.B. Kavan. "A Computer Based System for the Development and Analysis of Vocabulary Controlled Dictation Materials." Paper presented at the annual meeting of the American Educational Research Association, Washington, DC, April 1975.

186. Geoffrion, L.D., and R.D. Bergeron. "Initial Reading Through Computer Animation." Paper presented at the annual meeting of the American Educational Research Association, NY, April 1977.

187. ______, and E.P. Goldenberg. "Computer Based Exploratory Learning Systems for Communication Handicapped Children." Journal of Special Education 15 (1981): 325-332.

Individualized instruction and instructional management paradigms discussed.

188. Goldberg, L.M., and F.S. Rubin. "Interactive Computer Controlled TV for the Deaf." Audiovisual Instruction 23 (1978): 16-17.

Presents example of interactive communication model with the computer as a major interface. These devices allow students to monitor classroom activities and participate in all types of classroom activities.

189. Golton, R.F. "The Effects of Student Interaction on Computer Assisted Instruction in Mathematics at the Sixth Grade Level." Ph.D. dissertation. University of California, Berkeley, 1975.

190. Greenberg, J.C. "Effectiveness of Computer Assisted Videocassette Module For Reading Instruction." Ph.D. dissertation. University of Maryland, 1984.

191. Griswold, P.A. "Elementary Students' Attitudes During Two Years of Computer Assisted Instruction." American Educational Research Journal 21 (1984): 737-754.

Longitudinal study of attitudinal reactions towards computer technology reveals positive nature of technological interventions.

192. Gulian, E. "Vowel Learning and The Vowel System of Deaf Children: Age and Feedback Related Differences." Journal of Communication Disorders 16 (1983): 449-469.

Program to develop vowel learning with computer interface.

193. Guthrie, J.T. "Research: One Computer Literacy Skill." _Journal of Reading_ 24 (1981): 458-460.

Use of computer in developing research skills.

194. Haertel, G.D., H.J. Walberg, L. Junker, and E.T. Pascarella. "Early Adolescent Sex Differences in Science Learning: Evidence from the National Asssessment of Educational Progress." _American Educational Research Journal_ 9 (1981): 329-341.

Analyzes NAEP studies. Use of computers is still dominated by males. Notes fear of females being unable to gain entrance into career fields that use technology if this trend continues.

195. Harper, J.A., and N.J. Ewing. "A Comparison of the Effectiveness of Microcomputer and Workbook Instruction on Reading Comprehension Performance of High Incidence Handicapped Children." _Educational Technology_ 26 (1986): 140-145.

196. Hannafin, M.J. "Guidelines for Using Locus of Instructional Control in the Design of Computer Assisted Instruction." _Journal of Instructional Development_ 7 (1984): 6-10.

197. Harris, M.L. "The Perceptions of Selected Elementary and Secondary School Parents, Teachers and Building Administrators Regarding the Applications of Computer Technology in the Public Schools." Ph.D. dissertation. University of Nebraska, Lincoln, 1984.

198. Harris, R.T. "An Evaluation of Computer Assisted Instruction in Mathematics Using Test and Practice Method for Third and Sixth Grade Students." Ph.D. dissertation. United States International University, 1976.

199. Hauger, B.A. "A Comparison of Computer-Assisted Instruction and Teacher-Directed Instruction in Teaching Microcomputer Keyboarding to Sixth Graders. Ph.D. dissertation. University of North Dakota, 1986.

200. Hawley, S.C. "The Effect of Time Using Computer Assisted Instruction in a Remedial Mathematics Program upon Achievement and Attitudes in Students in Grades 6, 7,

8." Ph.D. dissertation. University of Cincinnati, 1984.

201. Hawkins, J. Computers and Girls: Rethinking the Issues. New York: Bank Street College Of Education, 1984.

Discusses ways in which female students can become active in computer learning and literacy.

202. ______, M. Hamolsky, and P. Heide. "Paired Problem Solving in a Computer Context." Paper presented at the annual meeting of the American Educational Research Association, New Orleans, April 1984.

203. ______, K. Sheingold, M. Gearhart, and C. Berger. "Microcomputers in Schools: Impact on the Social Life of Elementary Classrooms." Journal of Applied Developmental Psychology 3 (1982): 361-373.

Presents effects of technology in classroom life with emphasis on ways teachers use computers in social as well as academic settings.

204. Heap, J.L. "Collaborative Practices during Computer Writing in a First Grade Classroom." Paper presented at the annual meeting of the American Educational Research Association, San Francisco, 1986.

205. Hendon, C.A. "A Comparison of Reading and Vocabulary Achievement of Elementary Students Taught with Two Reading Teaching Methods." Ph.D. dissertation. University of Kansas, 1975.

206. Henney, M., and V. Boysen. "The Effect of Computer Simulation Training on the Ability To Administer an Informal Reading Inventory." Journal of Educational Research 72 (1979): 265-270.

Uses of computer to learn informal reading inventory are studied. Discusses transferability of learning and learning styles.

207. Hess, R.D., and I.T. Miura. Gender and Socioeconomic Differences in Enrollment in Computer Camps and Classes. Stanford: Stanford University School of Education, 1983.

Analyzes the educational implications of upper middle-class domination of computer camps and classes.

208. Hessemer, J.S. "The Effect of Computer-Assisted Instruction on Motivation in Fourth Grade Mathematics." Ph.D. dissertation. University of Pennsylvania, 1986.

209. Heuston, D.H. "Computers in Elementary and Secondary Education." ERIC ED 246 845, 1983.

210. Hickok, T.A. "Computer Education for Deaf Youngsters: A Mutual Effort by the University of California and The California School for the Deaf in Berkeley." Paper presented at the Association for The Development of Computer Based Instructional Systems Summer Meeting, Portland, ME, August 1975.

211. Hicks, B. _Students: Where the Action Is: Illinois Series in Educational Applications Of Computers_. State of Illinois Department of Education: Springfield, IL, 1975.

Case study of ways computers are being used in Illinois public schools. Types of uses range from compensatory education to advanced placement classes in high schools.

212. Hirsch, M.L. "The Effect of Computer Assisted Instruction in Problem Solving on the Cognitive Abilities of Fifth Grade Students." Ph.D. dissertation. United States International University, 1986.

213. Hoffman, J.T. "Reading Achievement and Attitude Toward Reading of Elementary Students Receiving Supplementary Computer Instruction Compared with Students Receiving Supplementary Traditional Instruction." Ph.D. dissertation. Ball State University, 1984.

214. Houser, L.L., and C.R. Trueblood. "Transfer of Learning on Similar Metric Conversion Tasks." _Journal of Educational Research_ 68 (1975): 235-237.

Discussion of computers in learning metrics.

215. Howey, C.L. "The Effects of Different Feedback Strategies on The Attitude of Students Involved in Computer Assisted Instruction." Ph.D. dissertation. Wayne State University, 1983.

216. Huenergard, C., and G. Albertson. "A Computer Application for Severely Handicapped Children." ERIC ED 245 466, 1984.

217. Hunter, B. "Computer Literacy in the K-8 Curriculum." Phi Delta Kappan 65 (1983): 115-118.

Analyzes ways to integrate computer literacy throughout the curriculum. Calls for components of computer literacy to be spread throughout the curriculum rather than in in one designated area.

218. Indian Affiliates, Inc. "Computer-Aided Instruction in Education Basics for Indian Students." ERIC ED 247 054, 1983.

219. Jacobson, E., and M. Thompson. "Self Managed Learning Using CAI." Paper presented at the annual meeting of the American Educational Research Association, Washington, DC, Apri 1975.

220. Jacoby, A. "Word Processing with Elementary School Students--A Teaching and Learning Experience for Both Teachers and Students." ERIC ED 246 449, 1984.

221. Jennings, M.H. Foundation. "Results of Computer Assisted Instruction at Bath Elementary School." ERIC ED 195 245, 1979.

222. Johnson, D. "On-Line Diagnosis Of Reading Difficulties IV." ERIC ED 162 227, 1978.

223. Johnson, E.L. "Computing and Handicapped Education." Educational Computer 4 (1984): 27-28.

Presents ways in which computers assist handicapped youngsters.

224. Joiner, L.M., G.J. Vensel, J.D. Ross, and B.J. Silverstein. Microcomputers in Education. Holmes Beach, FL: Learning Publications, 1982.

Overview of ways microcomputers are currently being used in educational settings.

225. Karr, L.G. "The Effects of Token Reinforcement in a Computer Assisted Instruction Program." Ph.D. dissertation. Texas A&M University, 1978.

226. Kern, R. "Individualizing Educational Strategies: An APPLE Computer Managed System for the Diagnosis and Evaluation of Reading, Math and Behavior." Journal of Reading, Writing and Learning Disabilities International 1 (1985): 139-145.

Presents use of computer in diagnosis of the types of methodologies that would be most successful for individual students.

227. Kim, Y.S. "The Effect of Prescribed Versus Student-Controlled Instructional Sequences on Knowledge Using CAI and Piagetian Developmental Theory." Ph.D. dissertation. Columbia University Teachers College, 1986.

228. King, M.H. "The Impact of Computer Assisted Instruction on the Acquisition of English As a Second Language." Ph.D. dissertation. United States International University, 1985.

229. Kleiman, G. "Microcomputers and Hyperactive Children." Creative Computing 5 (1981): 227-228.

Example of using microcomputers in treatment of hyperactive children.

230. Koenig, A.J. "Developing Writing and Word Processing Skills with Visually Impaired Children: A Beginning." Journal of Visual Impairment and Blindness 79 (1985): 308-310.

Presents use of computers with visually impaired children. Emphasizes ways to integrate braille skills and writing skills.

231. Korotkin, A.L. A Study of the Use of Computers in the Development of Science Career Awareness in Elementary School Children. Rockville, MD: Montgomery County, 1978.

Programs using science as they influence children and career choice.

232. Kosberb, B. "Andrus Instructional Management System: Identifying School Behavior Problems." Paper presented at the annual convention of the Council for Exceptional Children, Washington, DC, April 1978.

233. Kraus, W.H. "Using a Computer Game To Reinforce Skills in Addition Basic Facts in Second Grade." Journal for Research in Mathematics Education 12 (1981): 152-155.

Drill programs and their effectiveness in presenting basic skill facts.

234. Kulik, C., K. Kulik, and R.L. Bangert-Downs. "Effects of Computer Based Education on Elementary School Pupils." A symposium paper presented at the annual meeting of the American Educational Research Association, New Orleans, April 1984.

235. Lally, M. "Computer-Assisted Teaching of Sight Word Recognition for Mentally Retarded School Children." American Journal Of Mental Deficiency 85 (1981): 383-388.

Effectiveness of computer and sight reading programs. At this point they seem to be an efficient way to present materials.

236. Lance, W.D. "Use of Microcomputers in Special Education: A Survey of Special Education Teachers in the Saddleback Valley Unified School District." ERIC ED 253 028, 1984.

237. Lanese, J. "Computer Assisted Instruction In Mathematics." ERIC ED 236 295, 1983.

238. Lang, M. "The Social Effects of Competitive and Cooperative Video Games on Six and Seven Year Old Boys." Ph.D. dissertation. University of Alabama, 1984.

239. Langer, J.A. "Computer Technology and Reading Instruction: Perspectives and Directions." ERIC ED 214 131, 1982.

240. Laudato, N.C. "The Design and Development of a Computer Assisted Instructional Program in Word Problem Solving for the Elementary School." Ph.D. dissertation. University of Pittsburgh, 1975.

241. Laudato, N.C., and R.A. Roman. "Computer Assisted Instruction in Word Problems: Design and Assessment." Paper presented at the annual meeting of the American Educational Research Association, Washington, DC, April 1975.

242. Lavin, R., and J. Sanders. Longitudinal Evaluation of the C/A/I Computer Assisted Instruction Title I Project: 1979-1982. Chelmsford, MA: Merrimack Education Center, 1983.

Use of computers in compensatory education programs. Seems to be an effective/cost efficient way to deliver instruction.

243. Levin, J.A., and M.J. Bourta. "Writing with Computers in Classrooms: "You Get EXACTLY the Right Amount of Space!" Theory into Practice 22 (1983): 291-295.

Presents writing and use of word processing programs in teaching writing skills in a positive light. Of particular note are the positive student reactions in preparing compositions with word processing programs.

244. ______, M.J. Bourta, and M. Vasconellos. "Microcomputer Based Environments for Writing: A Writer's Assistant." Classroom Computers and Cognitive Science. Edited by A. Wilkinson. New York: Academic Press, 1983.

Ways to effectively use computers in the teaching of writing skills.

245. Levy, C. "A Comparative Study of the Reading Achievement Of Pupils Exposed To Computer Assisted Reading Instruction, Prescriptive Reading Instruction, and Traditional Reading Instruction." Ph.D. dissertation. Texas Southern University, 1982.

246. Levy, M.H. "An Evaluation of Computer Assisted Instruction upon the Achievement of Fifth Grade Students As Measured by Standardized Tests." Ph.D. dissertation. University of Bridgeport, 1985.

247. Lewis, J., and R. Adank. "The Relationship Between Attitudes Towards School and Achievement for Groups of Elementary School Children Exposed to Two Models of Instruction." Educational and Psychological Measurement 35 (1975): 503-505.

Presents use of the computer as part of an instructional model as compared to traditional classroom. Computer proves to be effective, but not in all learning environments especially those involving higher level thinking skills.

248. Lewis, M.A. "A Study of the Effects of Competitive and Individualistic Feedback on Children's Attributional Perceptions and Performance in Computer Assisted Mathematics Instruction." Ph.D. dissertation. University of Northern Colorado, 1985.

249. Lieberman, D. "Children and Computers: Patterns of Use and Orientation Towards Reading." Paper presented at the annual meeting of the International Communication Association, San Francisco, June 1984.

250. ______. "Research on Children and Microcomputers: A Review of Utilization and Effects Studies." <u>Microcomputers and Children: Research on the Newest Medium</u>. Edited by M. Chen and W. Paisley. Beverly Hills, CA: Sage, 1985.

How computers are used in schools and ways that they are most effective.

251. Linn, M.C. "The Cognitive Consequences of Programming Instruction in Classrooms." <u>Educational Researcher</u> 14 (1985): 14-29.

Presents carryover effects of programming instruction.

252. Lockheed, M.E., J. Gulovsen, and S. Morse. <u>Observations of Computer Using Students</u>. Cambridge, MA: Harvard Graduate School of Education, Educational Technology Center, 1985.

Ways in which students use computers both academically and socially.

253. Louie, S. "Locus of Control Among Computer Using Children. A Report of a Pilot Study." ERIC ED 260 692, 1985.

254. Lysiak, F. "Computer Assisted Instruction, 1975-76 Evaluation Report, A Title I Program." ERIC ED 140 495, 1976.

255. Macken, E., and P. Suppes. "Evaluation Studies on CCC Elementary School Curriculums 1971-75." CCC Educational Studies 1 (1976): 2-14.

Early studies of CAI in elementary schools (1-6) document effectiveness. These early programs focused on drill and practice skills in basic skill areas.

256. Marsh, M. "Computer Assisted Instruction in Reading." Journal of Reading 26 (1983): 697-701.

Overview of ways CAI is being used in reading instruction.

257. Martin, J.H. "An Eclectic Approach to Reading." School Administrator 41 (1984): 18-19.

Use of computers in a reading program.

258. Maser, A.L. "Highline Public Schools Computer Assisted Instruction Project: A Program To Meet Disadvantaged Students' Individual Needs for Basic Skill Development." ERIC ED 167 114, 1977.

259. Mason, E.J. "Evaluation of IST Courses. FY 81 Pilot Study." ERIC ED 229 003, 1981.

260. Mason, G.E. "Advantages and Didsadvantages of the Computer As a Teacher of Reading." Paper presented at the annual meeting of the National Reading Conference, Clearwater Beach, FL, December 1981.

261. ______, and J.S. Blanchard. Computer Applications In Reading. International Reading Association: Newark, DE: 1979.

Highlights use of computers on a national level in teaching reading skills.

262. Mason, M.M.T. "A Longitudinal Study of the Effects of Computer Assisted Instruction on the Mathematics Achievement of the Learning Disabled and Educable Mentally Retarded." Ph.D. dissertation. University of Iowa, 1984.

263. Mawby, R., C. Clements, R.D. Pea, and J. Hawkins. <u>Structured Interviews on Children's Conceptions of Computers</u>. New York: Bank Street College of Education, 1984.

Children's perceptions of computer technology and its usefulness in their education.

264. May, B.A. "Effective Instruction for Teaching Basic Skills with Computer Assisted Language Learning in an English As a Second Language Program." Ph.D. dissertation. Texas A&I University, 1984.

265. McCahill, P. "CAI in ESL: One Approach That Has Worked." <u>TESL Talk</u> 14 (1983): 65-71.

Use of computers in an ESL program.

266. McClurg, P.A. "A Study of the Effects of Playing Selected Microcomputer Games on the Spatial Ability of Fifth, Seventh and Ninth Grade Males and Females." Ph.D. dissertation. University of Oregon, 1985.

267. Meister, G.R. <u>Successful Integration of Microcomputers in an Elementary School</u>. Stanford, CA: Institute for Research on Educational Finance and Governance, Stanford University, 1984.

Ways to integrate computers in an elementary school.

268. Merrell, L.E. "The Effects of Computer Assisted Instruction on the Cognitive Ability of Third, Fourth and Fifth Grade Students." Ph.D. dissertation. East Texas State University, 1984.

269. Metrics Associates, Inc. "Evaluation of the Computer Assisted Title I Project, 1980-81." ERIC ED 233 122, 1981.

270. ______. "Longitudinal Evaluation of the C/A/I Computer Assisted Instruction Title I Project, 1979-1982." ERIC ED 234 062, 1983.

271. Metzger, M. "The Influence of Microcomputer Assisted Instruction upon the Spelling of Children Diagnosed As Learning Disabled." Ph.D. dissertation. University of Oregon, 1984.

272. Mevarech, Z.R., and Y. Rich. "Effects of Computer Assisted Mathematics Instruction on Disadvantaged Pupils' Cognitive and Affective Development." Journal of Educational Research 79 (1985): 5-11.

Successful ways in which computers are used in low socioeconomic level schools and how students perceive them as part of the instructional process.

273. Miller, D.M. "Retention of Art Concepts: Effects of Advanced Organizers, Objectives and Inserted Questions In High School Computer Assisted Instruction and Booklets." Ph.D. dissertation. Northern Illinois University, 1979.

274. Miller, J.D., Jr. "The Effect of Computer Assisted Problem Solving Instruction on the Academic Achievement of Elementary Students." Ph.D. dissertation. United States International University, 1985.

275. Miller, L. "Computers and the Language Arts." Paper presented at the Colloquium on Canadian Research in Reading and Language Arts in Canada, Lethbridge, Alberta, June 1984.

276. Miller, S.W.H. "A Comparison of Computer Assisted Instruction with Prescription Learning and the Traditional "Pull-Out" Program Used in Supplementing Instruction of Mathematics Basic Skills to Chapter I (Title I) Students." Ph.D. dissertation. Oregon State University, 1984.

277. Millman, P.G. "The Effects of Computer Assisted Instruction on Attention Deficits, Achievement, and Attitudes of Learning Disabled Children." Ph.D. dissertation. University of Virginia, 1984.

278. Mitchell, E. "Home Video Games: Children and Parents Learn To Play and Play To Learn." Paper presented at the annual meeting of the American Educational Research Association, New Orleans, April 1984.

279. Mothner, H., and J. Shawn. "Microcomputers Are 'Macrocontributors' to Special Education Programs." American Annals of the Deaf 127 (1982): 449-451.

Examples of positive ways computers contribute to the education of special education children. Especially noteworthy is the ability to track and manage student IEP's (individual education plans).

280. Neufield, H.H. "Reading, Writing and Algorithms: Computer Literacy in the Schools." ERIC ED 211 959, 1982.

281. Nickerson, R.S. "Computer Programming As a Vehicle for Teaching Thinking Skills." Thinking: The Journal of Philosophy for Children 4 (1982): 42-48.

Computer programming as part of teaching critical and logical thinking tasks.

282. Nicolay, W.L. "Group Learning and the Computer: The Teacher Brings an APPLE for the Students." Thinking: The Journal of Philosophy for Children 5 (1983): 42-48.

Use of the computer as part of a group problem solving process.

283. Niemiec, R.P. "The Meta-Analysis of Computer Assisted Instruction at the Elementary School Level." Ph.D. dissertation. University of Illinois-Chicago, 1984.

284. Nomeland, R.E., and R. Harris. "Computer Assisted Instruction at Kendall Demonstration Elementary School." Paper presented at the Association for the Development of Computer Based Instructional Systems Summer Conference, Minneapolis, August 1976.

285. Olson, D. "Culture, Technology and Intellect." The Nature of Intelligence. Edited by L. Resnick and R. Glaser. Potomac, MD: Erlbaum, 1976.

Ways in which technology affects the nature of the intellectual processes.

286. O'Neal, F. "Waterford School and the WICAT Education Institute: An Alternative Model for CAI and Development Research." CALICO Journal 1 (1983): 19-23.

Immersion of CAI in a school environment through the introduction of computers at all grade, age, and curricular levels and how research studies have been developed to track the results of this experimental school.

287. Ortmann, L.N. "The Effectiveness of Supplementary Computer Assisted Instruction in Reading at the 4-6 Grade Level. Ph.D. dissertation. University of the Pacific, 1983

288. Paisley, W. "Children, New Media and Microcomputers: Continuities of Research." *Children and Microcomputers: Research on the Newest Medium*. Edited by M. Chen and W. Paisley. Beverly Hills, CA: Sage, 1985.

Research in other media as well as computers, parallels, and similar problems presented.

289. ______, and M. Chen. *Children and Electronic Texts: Challenges and Opportunities of the New Literacy*. Palo Alto, CA: The Institute for Communication Research, Stanford University, 1982.

Processing and skill differential developments between electronic and paper texts.

290. Passow, H.A. "Curricula for the Gifted." *National/State Leadership Training Institute on the Gifted and Talented*. Ventura, CA: Ventura County Superintendent of Schools Office, 1982.

Ways in which to use computers in programs for the gifted.

291. Piele, D.T. "Microcomputers "GOTO" School." Paper presented at the annual meeting of the American Educational Research Association, San Francisco, April 1979.

292. Piper, K.L. "Beyond Basic Skills: Using the Microcomputer To Extend Basic Skills Instruction in the Language Arts." Paper presented at the annual meeting of the National Council of the Teachers of English, Denver, November 1983.

293. Pogrow, S., and B. Buchanan. "Higher Order Thinking for Compensatory Students." *Educational Leadership* 43 (1985): 40-43.

Computers and their uses in compensatory education programs that teach higher order thinking skills.

294. Polsgrove, L. "The Use of CATTS Methodology for Teaching Children Self Control." ERIC ED 159 869, 1977.

295. Poore, J.H., and J.W. Hamblen. "Improvement of Basic Mathematical Skills with PLATO: An Experiment." AEDS Journal (Summer, 1983): 23-31.

Presents PLATO math skill program effectiveness.

296. ______, J.E. Qualls, and B.L. Brown. "The Educational Effectiveness and Economics of Delivery of the PLATO Basic Skills Mathematics Lessons: A Field Study." AEDS Journal 14 (Fall, 1981): 48-59.

Analyzes use of a CAI program in terms of both its effectiveness in delivering instruction as well as its cost effectiveness versus traditional methods.

297. Post, P.E. "The Effect of Students' Field Independence/Field Dependence on Computer Assisted Instruction Achievement." Ph.D. dissertation. Purdue University, 1984.

298. Poulsen, G., and E. Macken. Evaluation Studies of CCC Elementary School Curriculum, 1975-1977. Palo Alto, CA: Computer Curriculum Corporation, 1978.

Early studies of CAI and its effect in increasing cognitive development in an elementary school environment.

299. Prinz, P.M., and K.E. Nelson. "A Child-Computer-Teacher Interactive Method for Teaching Reading to Young Deaf Children." ERIC ED 247 720, 1984.

300. Ragosta, M. The ETS-LAUSD Computer Assisted Instruction Project: Does CAI Work? Princeton: Educational Testing Service, 1981.

Use of computers in Los Angeles School District. Ways in which CAI benefited students.

301. ______, D.W. Holland, and D.T. Jamison. The ETS/LAUSD Study. The Final Report. Princeton: Educational Testing Service, 1982.

Update of item #300.

302. Rapides Parish School Board. "Individualized Reading Instruction for Students Computer Managed Reading System. Validation report." ERIC ED 127 552, 1975.

303. Reisner, E.R. "The Use of Computers in Instruction Supported Under Chapter 1 of the Education Consolidation and Improvement Act." ERIC ED 238 404, 1983.

304. Rosegrant, T. "Using The Microcomputer As a Tool for Learning To Read and Write." Journal of Learning Disabilities 18 (1984): 113-115.

Presents effectiveness of computer in reading/writing programs.

305. Roth, S., and I.L. Beck. "Research and Instructional Issues Related to the Enhancement of Children's Decoding Skills Through a Microcomputer Program. Paper presented at the annual meeting of the American Educational Research Association, New Orleans, April 1984.

306. Rowe, N. "Grammar As a Programming Langauge." ERIC ED 204 812, 1976.

307. Sandals, L.H. "Computer Assisted Applications for Learning with Special Needs Children." Paper presented at the annual meeting of the American Educational Research Association, San Francisco, April 1979.

308. Saracho, O.N. "The Effects of a Computer Assisted Instruction Program on Basic Skills Achievement and Attitudes Towards Instruction of Spanish Speaking Migrant Children." American Educational Research Journal 19 (1982): 201-219.

Seminal work on effectiveness of CAI in second language programs. Results indicate that CAI is extremely useful in increasing knowledge of basic skills and in interesting students to stay in school.

309. Sedlacek, C.J. "A Study Comparing Achievement and Attitude Differences in Fifth Grade Remedial Reading Students Taught Using Computer Assisted Instruction and Conventional Management Programs." Ph.D. dissertation. University of Alabama, 1984.

310. Seidman, R.H. "The Effects of Learning a Computer Programming Language on the Logical Reasoning of School Children." Paper presented at the annual meeting of the American Educational Research Association, Los Angeles, April 1981.

311. Shanahan, S.M. "Computer-Assisted Instruction and the Creative Thinking and Writing Abilities of Fourth Grade Students." Ph.D. dissertation. Oklahoma State University, 1986.

312. Shiengold, K., J. Hawkins, and C. Char. "I'm the Thinkest, You're the Typist": The Interaction of Technology and the Social Life of Classrooms." <u>Journal of Social Issues</u> 40 (1984): 49-62.

Analyzes and presents integration of technology and classroom life.

313. Shu, J. "Acquisition of Arithmetic Understanding As A Skill in Relation to Method of Instruction." Ph.D. dissertation. Indiana University, 1983.

314. Silfen, R., and A.C. Howes. "A Summer Reading Program With CAI: An Evaluation." <u>Computers, Reading and Langauge Arts</u> 1 (1984): 20-22.

Ways to use computers as part of a reading development program.

315. Simmons, L.N. <u>Effects Of Educational Technology: A Review of the Literature</u>. Dallas Independent School District, Dallas, 1975.

Presentation of series of research studies involving use of CAI in schools.

316. Sisson, L.H. "Evaluating Children's Learning Disabilities with an APPLE II Personal Computer or Tempting

Poor Learners with an Apple." Paper presented at the annual meeting of the Western Psychological Association, San Francisco, April 1983.

317. Snelbecker, G.E. "Impact of Computers and Electronic Technology on the Teaching Methodologies and the Learning Process." Journal of Children in Contemporary Society 14 (1981): 43-53.

Discussion of changes in classrooms as a result of the introduction of computer technology.

318. SRA Technologies, Inc., and COSMOS Corporation. Microcomputers in the Schools: Implementation in Special Education. Arlington, VA: SRA Technologies, 1983.

Overview of ways computers are being used in special education classrooms nationwide.

319. Steele, K.J. "The Effect of Microcomputer Assisted Instruction on the Computer Literacy of Fifth Grade Students." Journal of Educational Research 76 (1983): 298-301.

Uses of CAI in teaching computer literacy. Results indicate a positive correlation in use of CAI and gain in computer literacy.

320. ______, M.T. Battista, and G.H. Krockover. "The Effect of Microcomputer Instruction upon the Computer Literacy of High Ability Students." Gifted Child Quarterly 26 (1982): 162-164.

Study of use of computers with gifted students. Results indicate a positive acceptance of the technology.

321. Steinberg, E.R. "Using PLATO To Teach Problem Solving." ERIC ED 202 455, 1980.

322. Stewart, W.J. "Diagnosing-Remediating Mathematics Difficulties Through The Computer." Journal of Mathematics and Science Teaching 3 (1984): 12-13.

Ways to use computers in locating and remediating mathematical difficulties.

323. Stuzman, C. "Computer Supported Instruction in California Elementary and Secondary Schools." Paper presented at the annual meeting of The Fresno Research Association, Fresno, CA, 1981.

324. Suppes, P. "Performance Models of American Indian Students on Computer Assisted Instruction in Elementary Mathematics." Instructional Science 4 (1975): 303-314.

Descriptive report of CAI as an instructional model. Results indicate positive student performance.

325. Swinton, S.S., M. Amarel, and J.A. Morgan. The PLATO Elementary Demonstration Educational Outcome Final Evaluation: Final Report, Summary and Conclusions. Princeton, NJ: Educational Testing Service, 1978.

Report on use of PLATO to teach basic skills. Successful implementation indicated.

326. Taitt, N.P. "The Effect of Computer Programming Instruction on the Problem Solving Ability of Pre-Service Elementary Teachers." Ph.D. dissertation. University of Illinois - Champaign/Urbana, 1985.

327. Tamborine, R. "Effects of Questions, Personalized Communication Style, and Pauses for Reflection in Children's Educational Programs." Journal of Educational Research 79 (1985): 19-26.

Discussion of ways that questions and individualized instructional paradigms can increase cognitive development.

328. Tawney, J.W. "Programming Educational Environments for the Severely Retarded: Curriculum Development, Research and Service, Emanating from an Errorless Learning Model." Paper presented at the World Congress On The Future of Special Education, Stirling, Scotland, June 1978.

329. Taylor, R.P. The Computer in School: Tutor, Tool, Tutee. New York: Teachers College Press, 1980.

Classic work on ways computers might be used in school settings.

330. Taylor, S.S. "The Effects of Mastery, Adaptive Mastery, and Non-Mastery Models on the Learning of a Mathematical Task." Paper presented at the annual meeting of the American Educational Research Association, Washington, DC, April 1975.

331. Tharp, A.L., and W.E. Robbins. "Using Computers in a Natural Language Mode for Elementary Education." International Journal of Man - Machine Studies 7 (1975): 703-726.

Natural langauge programming (English) for elementary education students. Notes results in increasing ability to develop programming skills.

332. Thomas, R., and B. Gustafson. "The Design, Development and Evaluation of a Low Cost Computer Managed Spelling System." AEDS Journal 16 (1983): 168-176.

Development of spelling management program for elementary schools.

333. Thompson, B.J. "Computers in Reading: A Review of Applications and Implications." Educational Technology 9 (1980): 168-176.

Ways computers are being used in reading instruction including skill and content development.

334. Thompson, M. "Beyond the Computer: Reading As a Process of Intellectual Development." Computers, Reading and Language Arts 2 (1985): 13-15.

Use of the computer as part of the reading and language development process.

335. Tittnick, E.M., and N. Brown. "Positive and Negative Uses of Technology in Human Interactions." Young Children in a Computerized Environment. Edited by M. Frank. New York: Haworth Press, 1982.

Overview of positive and negative implications of uses of technology in school settings.

336. Trachtman, P. "Putting Computers into the Hands of Children Without Language." Smithsonian 14 (1984): 42-50.

Use of computers with langauge disabled children in a variety of traditional and nontraditional educational settings. Disabled children responded positively to computers.

337. Trowbridge, D., and R. Durnin. *Results from an Investigation of Groups Working at the Computer*. Unpublished manuscript, Univerity of California, Irvine, 1983.

Group learning as part of computer interactions viewed in a positive light.

338. Turner, G.Y. "A Comparison of Computer Assisted Instruction and a Programmed Instructional Booklet in Teaching Selected Phonics Skills to Preservice Teachers." Ph.D. dissertation. University of Arkansas, 1983.

339. University of Pittsburgh Learning Research and Development Center. *The Development of Microcomputer Assistance to Instruction in Reading and Verbal Skills: Six Month Report to the Buhl Foundation*. Pittsburgh, PA: University of Pittsburgh, 1982.

Beginning project report indicates computer can be of assistance in development of language skills.

340. Venezky, R.L. "On-Line Diagnosis Of Reading Difficulties." ERIC ED 106 765, 1975.

341. ______. "Summary Of Studies for an On-Line Reading Diagnosis System III." ERIC ED 138 967, 1977.

342. Vincent, B.R. "The Effect of a Dynamically Adaptive Computer Model on Multiple Discrimination Learning." Ph.D. dissertation. Brigham Young University, 1985.

343. Von Feldt, J.R. *A National Survey of the Use of Computer Assisted Instruction in Schools for the Deaf*. National Technical Institute for the Deaf: Rochester, NY: 1978.

Ways computers are being used to assist in education of hearing impaired children.

344. Walker, R.J. "An Update on Computers in the Classroom." ERIC ED 203 849, 1980.

345. Warash, B.G. "Computer Language Experience Approach." Paper presented at the annual meeting of the National Council of the Teachers of English, Spring Conference, Washington, DC, April 1980.

346. Warner, T.D. "The Effects of Computer Based Education on Sixth Grade Students' Self-Concept, Locus of Control, and Mathematics Achievement." Ph.D. dissertation. University of Akron, 1981.

347. Wartella, A., and B. Reeves. "Recurring Issues in Research on Children and Media." Educational Technology 23 (1983): 5-9.

Overview of research questions being studied in various media contexts including computers.

348. Watkins, B., and D. Brimm. "The Adoption and Use of Microcomputers in Homes and Elementary Schools." Children and Microcomputers: Research on the Newest Medium. Edited by M. Chen and W. Paisley. Beverly Hills, CA: Sage, 1985.

Ways that computers are being used in school and home settings, who is using them and, why they are being used.

349. Watkins, M., and S. Abram. "Reading CAI with First Grade Students." The Computing Teacher 12 (1985): 43-45.

Use of CAI in early elementary grades as a positive force in teaching reading skills.

350. ______, and C. Webb. "Computer Assisted Instruction with Learning Disabled Students." Educational Computer Magazine 1 (1981): 24-27.

Descriptive report on uses of CAI with the learning disabled.

351. Webb, N.M. "Microcomputer Learning in Small Groups: Cognitive Requirements and Group Processes." Journal of Educational Psychology 76 (1984): 1076-1088.

Small group interactions with computers. Affective as well as effective descriptions provided. Computers seem to work well in small (3) groups with divergent cognitive development.

352. Wertz, F.C. "Teaching Blissymbols with the Aid of the APPLE II Computer." Paper presented at the council for Exceptional Children National Conference on the use of Microcomputers in Special Education, Hartford, CT: March 1983.

353. Wesley, B.E. "The Effects of Computer Assisted Instruction and Locus of Control upon Preservice Elementary Teachers' Acquisition of Computer Literacy and the Integrated Science Skills." Ph.D. dissertation. Purdue University, 1983.

354. Whitson, S.K. "The Development of Melodic Concepts in Elementary School Age Children Using Computer-Assisted Instruction as a Supplemental Tool." Ph.D. dissertation. Ohio State University, 1986.

355. Williams, F., J. Coulombe, and L. Lievrouw. "Children's Attitudes Toward Small Computers: A Preliminary Study." _Educational Communication and Technology Journal_ 31 (1983): 3-7.

Discusses attitudes towards technology and its development.

356. ______, and V. Williams. _Microcomputers in Elementary Education: Perspectives On Implementation_. Belmont, CA: Wadsworth, 1984.

Overview of ways computers are being used in instructional interactions in elementary education.

357. Wilson, M.L.P. "The Development of CAI Programs for Teaching Music Fundamentals to Undergraduate Elementary Education Music Methods Classes." Ph.D. dissertation. Louisiana State University and Agricultural and Mechanical College, 1981.

358. Winters, J.J., Jr. "The Instructional Use of CAI in the Education of the Mentally Retarded." Paper presented at the World Congress on the Future of Special Education, Stirling, Scotland, June 1978.

359. Wolf, D.P. "Flexible Texts: Computer Editing in the Study of Writing." _Children and Computers. New Directions For Child Development. No. 28_. Edited by E.L. Klein. San Francisco: Jossey-Bass, 1985.

Use of computers and word processing in the develoment of writing and editing skills shows that children's writing skills are enhanced through computer usage.

360. Yin, R.K., and J.L. White. "Microcomputer Implementation in Schools: Findings from Twelve Case Studies." _Children and Microcomputers: Research on the Newest Medium_. Edited by M. Chen and W. Paisley. Beverly Hills, CA: Sage, 1985.

Description of ways computers are being used in a variety of school settings.

361. Zuk, D., and F. Danner. "The Effects of Microcomputers on Children's Attention to Reading Tasks." Paper presented at the annual meeting of the American Educational Research Association, San Francisco, 1986.

Secondary Education

362. Aaron, R. "Computer Managed Instruction for Behaviorally Disordered Adolescents." Reading Improvement 12 (1975): 103-107.

Discussion of methodology for using computers with troubled adolescents.

363. Aiello, N., and L.M. Wolfe. "A Meta-Analysis of Individualized Instruction in Science." Paper presented at the annual meeting of the American Educational Research Association, Boston, April 1980.

364. Alderman, D.L. Evaluation of the TICCIT Computer Assisted Instructional System in the Community College. Princeton: Educational Testing Service, 1978.

Positive indications for early CAI system. Implications for carryover effects for secondary schools developing management systems.

365. Anandam, K., E. Eisel, and L. Kotler. "Effectiveness of a Computer Based Feedback System for Writing." Journal of Computer Based Instruction 6 (1980): 125-133.

Ways computers can assist in teaching writing as measured by success in developing critique system from commentaries. Students' responses to this experiment were judged positive.

366. Anderson, S.J. "TICCIT Project." Paper presented at the annual meeting of the National Association of Educational Broadcasters, Chicago, October 1976.

367. Appleby, B.C. Computers and Composition: An Overview. ERIC ED 240 546, 1983.

368. Argento, B.J. Alternative Education Models Preliminary Findings of the Job Corps Educational Improvement Effort. Department of Labor: Washington, DC, 1980.

Ways Job Corps used CAI in teaching a variety of students at differing cognitive levels.

369. Askalini, M., and P. Thompson. "Report from the National Specialized Center Computer Assisted Instruction in Economics. Paper presented at the annual meeting of Economic Educators, Honolulu, October 1981.

370. Bailey, A.E. "The Effect of Computer Managed Instruction on Student Achievement in Mathematics." Ph.D. dissertation. Wayne State University, 1983.

371. Bangert, R.L., J.A. Kulik, and C.L.C. Kulik. "Individualized Systems of Instruction in Secondary Schools." Review of Educational Research 53 (1983): 143-158.

Computers discussed as one of the ways to individualize instruction.

372. Barker, B.O., and P.D. Petersen. "A Research Report of Small High Schools in the United States in Regards to Curricular Offerings, Microcomputer Use and Correspondence Courses." ERIC ED 239 825, 1984.

373. Beach, R., and A. Vacca. "Administrative Variables and Microcomputer Implementation: A Survey of High School Principals." Computers in the Schools 2 (1985): 31-46.

Different ways to implement uses of microcomputers.

374. Beaulieu, J.E. "A Study of the Effects of Selected Feedback Delay Intervals upon Retention of Science Material in a Computer Assisted Instructional Task with Junior High School Students." Ph.D. dissertation. University of Oregon, 1985.

375. Beck, J.J., Jr. "Extent Of Computer Use in Secondary Schools: The Texas Story." ERIC ED 226 712, 1982.

376. Bell, F.H. "Implementing Instructional Computing and Computer Literacy in a School or College." AEDS Journal 15 (1982): 169-176.

Suggests ways uses of computers might be introduced in schools and universities.

377. Blomeyer, R.L., Jr. Computer Based Foreign Language Instruction in Illinois: A Review of Literature, Some Preliminary Observations, and Recommendations for Consideration by the Illinois State Board of Eduction. Illinois State Board of Education: Springifield, IL, 1983.

Description of ways computer technology is being used in foreign language instruction.

378. Blood, D.G. "An Investigation of the Effects of Implementing "Basic Stuff" in Secondary School Physical Education Classes." Ph.D. dissertation. Illinois State University, 1984.

Uses of computers to teach introductory materials in physical education classes found to be effective.

379. Blume, G.W. "A Review of Research on the Effects of Computer Programming on Mathematical Problem Solving." Paper presented at the annual meeting of the American Educational Research Association, New Orleans, April 1984.

380. Boas, E.E., Jr. "An Analysis of Instructional Delivery Systems in Vocational Education Comparing Computer Managed-Instruction, Teacher-Delivered Module (Paper), and Lecture-Demonstration for the Same Instructional Module." Ph.D. dissertation. Temple University, 1979.

381. Bohrer, J. "Use of a Microcomputer in the Teaching of High School Mathematics." ERIC ED 211 071, 1981.

382. Bonner, J.F. "Beliefs of High School Principals Regarding Elements of Computer Literacy and Computer Uses in Their Schools." Ph.D. dissertation. University of Pennsylvania, 1986.

383. Bork, A. "Two Examples of Computer Based Learning on Personal Computers." AEDS Journal 14 (1983): 49-53.

Discuses individual and group learning using personal computers.

384. Bostrom, K. _An Evaluative Study of the Effects and Effectiveness of Microcomputer Based Teaching in Schools_. Social Science Research Council: London, 1982.

Discusses use of computers as an effective pedagogical tool in English schools.

385. Bosworth, K. "Adolescents, Health Education, and Computers: The Body Awareness Network (BARN)." _Health Education_ 14 (1983): 58-60.

Presents use of computers in health education.

386. Bowlsbey, J.H. _DISCOVER: A Computer Based Career Guidance and Counselor Administrative Support System. Field Trial Report_. DISCOVER Foundation, Inc.: Westminister, MD, 1976.

Analyzes career guidance system in which students obtain information about careers through key word input.

387. Bracey, G. "Computers in Education: What The Research Shows." _Electronic Learning_ 2 (1982): 51-54.

Overview of research studies describing computers and their effectiveness in school situations.

388. Bracey, G. "You Can Lead a Kid to Loiter, but You Can't Make Him Think." _Phi Delta Kappan_ 65 (1984): 644-647.

Discusses computers and their role in developing thinking skills.

389. Brangert-Drowns, R.L. "Effectiveness of Computer Based Education in Secondary School." _Journal of Computer Based Instruction_ 12 (1985): 59-68.

Study relating ways that computers can be used successfully in secondary schools through an integrated computer content curriculum model.

390. Brown, H.D. _Personnel Training--Secondary Vocational Agriculture Teacher Education_. Texas A&M University: College Station, TX, 1985.

Ways computers are used in vocational agriculture training.

391. Bukoski, W.J., and A.L. Korotkin. Computing Activities in Secondary Education. American Institute for Research in the Behavioral Sciences: Washington, DC, 1975.

Overview of uses of computers in nation's secondary schools.

392. ______. "Computing Activities in Secondary Education." Educational Technology 16 (1976): 9-22.

Discussion of methodologies, such as tutorials, for integrating computers in secondary school curriculums.

393. Burns, H.L., and G.H. Culp. "Stimulating Invention in English Composition Through Compuer Assisted Instruction." Educational Technology 20 (1980): 5-10.

Ways to stimulate thinking and writing processes through the use of computers.

394. Burns, P.K., and W.C. Bozeman. "Computer Assisted Instruction and Mathematics Achievement: Is There a Relationship?" Educational Technology 21 (1981): 32-39.

Positive report on uses of computers in mathematical instruction.

395. Burrowes, S.K. "A Study of the Effects of Using CAI to Teach Signed Numbers to Seventh Grade Gifted Students." Ph.D. dissertation. University of Akron, 1983.

396. California State Department of Education. Computer Literacy of California's Sixth and Twelfth Grade Students. California Assessment Program. California State Department of Education: Sacramento, CA, 1984.

Research status report on computer literacy in California schools after statewide computer literacy implementation mandates.

397. Camp, J.S., and G. Marchionini. "Computer Enhanced Mathematics." Viewpoints in Teaching and Learning 57 (1981): 1-12.

Pedagogical discussion of computers and mathematics.

398. Camp, W.G. Evaluation of Technology for the Vocational Classroom. Virginia Polytechnic Institute and State University: Blacksburg, VA, 1983.

Differing ways that computers are used in vocational education classrooms and their effectiveness.

399. Campbell, P.F. "The Effect of Programming Instruction in the High School on Performance in a University Level Programming Course." Paper presented at the meeting of the National Council of Teachers of Mathematics, Detroit, April 1983.

400. Carpenter, T.P., M.K. Corbitt, H.S. Knepner, Jr., M.M. Lindquist, and R.R. Reys. "The Current Status of Computer Literacy: NAEP Results for Secondary Students." Mathematics Teacher 73 (1980): 669-673.

401. Carter, K.P. "Evaluation of Computer Assisted Metric Instruction in a Ninth Grade Physical Science Program." Ph.D. dissertation. University of Texas at Austin, 1980.

402. Cepica, M.J. Integration of Computer Related Instruction in Texas Vocational Agriculture Programs. Final Report. Texas Technical University: Lubbock, TX, 1984.

Ways computers are used in vocational agriculture programs on a statewide basis.

403. Chambers, J.A., and A. Bork. Computer Assisted Learning in U.S. Secondary Schools. NY: Association for Computing Machinery, 1980.

Overview of status of computer usage in U.S. secondary schools including number of computers purchased, how computers are currently used, and prospects for the future.

404. Clark, R.D. "Handicapped Children and Computers." School Psychology Review 13 (1984): 461-468.

Positive report on ways computers can assist handicapped students.

405. Collins, A. "Effectiveness of an Interactive Map Display in Tutoring Geography." Journal of Educational Psychology 70 (1978): 1-7.

Presents geographical skill development using a computer model.

406. Condry, J., and D. Keith. "Educational and Recreational Uses of Computer Technology. Youth and Society 15 (1983): 87-112.

Video games, and computer use both in and out of school situations.

407. Conrath, M., and V. Mayer. "Microcomputers in Marine and Aquatic Education." Journal of Marine Education 6 (1985): 17-20.

Uses of microcomputers in the teaching of marine education.

408. Coombs, M.J., R. Gibson, and J.L. Alty. "Learning a First Computer Language: Strategies for Making Sense." International Journal of Man - Machine Studies 16 (1982): 449-486.

Ways to teach first computer languages.

409. Coople, C. "Computers in the Secondary Mathematics Curriculum." ERIC ED 204 144, 1981.

410. Cornelius, C.S. "A Comparison of Computer-Based Data Based Instruction and Retrieval Strategies with Traditional Instruction." Ph.D. dissertation. Pennsylvania State University, 1986.

411. Cornett, L.M. "Computers in Education: Implications for Schools and Colleges." Regional Spotlight 14 (1984): 1-13.

What large scale uses of microcomputer technology may mean for colleges and universities.

412. COSMOS Corporation. Microcomputers in the Schools. Implementation in Special Education. COSMOS Corporation: Washington, DC, 1983.

Status report on how computers are being used in nation's special education classrooms.

413. Cox, B.A. "Early Adolescent Use of Selected Problem-Solving Skills Using Microcomputers." Ph.D. dissertation. University of Michigan, Ann Arbor, 1980.

414. Crenshaw, H.M. II. "A Comparison of Two Computer Assisted Instruction Management Systems in Remedial Math." Ph.D. dissertation. Texas A&M University, 1982.

415. Crook, J.D. "Effects of Computer Assisted Instruction upon Seventh Grade Students' Growth in Writing Performance." Ph.D. dissertation. University of Nebraska-Lincoln, 1985.

416. Crosby, H.M. "The Effectiveness of the Instructional Use of Computers for Students with Mild Learning Problems: A Review of the Literature and Research." ERIC ED 249 688, 1983.

417. Cullem, T. "SAT Tutoring Programs: Give Them an Incomplete." Personal Computing 6 (1982): 128-129.

Effectiveness of SAT Tutorial programs presented.

418. Dalbey, J., and M. Linn. "Making Programming Instruction Cognitively Demanding." Paper presented at the annual meeting of the American Educational Research Association, New Orleans, April 1984.

419. Dalgaard, B.P. "Cost and Effectiveness Considerations in the Use of Computer Assisted Instruction in Economics." Journal of Economic Education 15 (1984): 309-323.

Analyzes pedagogical and economic costs of using CAI in economics classes.

420. Dalton, D.W. "A Comparison of the Effects of LOGO Use and Teacher-Directed Problem-Solving Instruction on the Problem-Solving Skills, Achievement and Attitudes of Low Average, and High Achieving Junior High School Learners." Paper presented at the annual convention of the Association for Educational Communications and Technology, Las Vegas, 1986.

421. Davis, J.E. "Correspondence Courses: A New Role in Rural Secondary Education." Rural Educator 5 (1983): 1-6.

Ways computers can be used in keeping track of correspondence courses.

422. Davis, R.B. "Alternative Uses of Computers in Schools: Cognitive vs. Natural Language Statements." Paper presented at the annual meeting of the American Educational Research Association, Boston, April 1980.

423. DiBlasio, M.K. "If and Where To Plug in the Computer: A Conceptual Framework for Computer Assisted Art." Studies in Art Education 25 (1983): 39-47.

424. Diem, R.A., and P.G. Fairweather. "An Evaluation of a Computer Assisted Education System in an Untraditional Academic Setting-a County Jail." AEDS Journal 13 (Spring, 1980): 204-212.

Discusses use of PLATO Basic Skills curriculum in a county jail and the implications for secondary education.

425. Disinger, J.F., and R.W. Fortner. Using Computers for Environmental Education. Information Bulletin No. 3. ERIC ED 260 907, 1984.

426. Dixon, P., and W. Judd. "A Comparison of Computer and Lecture Modes for Teaching Basic Statistics." Journal of Computer Based Instruction 4 (1977): 22-25.

Differential pedagogical strategies indicate computers are useful in certain segments of statistical classes.

427. Dominick, J.R. "Videogames, Television Violence, and Aggression in Teenagers." Journal of Communication 34 (1984): 136-147.

Discusses violence in video games and its effects on developing aggressive behavior.

428. Dorbin, D.N. "Limitations on the Use of Computers in Composition." Paper presented at the annual meeting of the conference on College Composition and Communication, Minneapolis, March 1985.

429. Dwyer, T.A. "Soloworks: Computer Based Laboratories for High School Mathematics." School Science and Mathematics 22 (1975): 93-99.

Ways to teach mathematics in a laboratory setting.

430. Educational Technology Center. The Use of Information Technologies for Education in Science, Mathematics, and Computers. An Agenda For Research. Cambridge, MA: Educational Technology Center, 1984.

Description of research possibilities in schools using computer and microcomputer technology.

431. Edwards, D.H. "A Survey To Establish Present Level of Computer Education in Missouri Middle Schools and Junior High Schools." Ph.D. dissertation. St. Louis University, 1984.

432. Elliott, P.H., and P.G. Watson. "A Research Agenda for the Model Secondary School for the Deaf: TICCIT System." Paper presented at the Association for the Development of Computer Based Instructional Systems Summer Conference, Minneapolis, August 1976.

433. Engel, C.W., and H.E. Payne, Jr. "Computer Simulation in Secondary School Mathematics." Viewpoints in Teaching and Learning 57 (1981): 114-128.

Ways computers are used in a simulation mode to teach mathematics.

434. Engel, F.L., and J.J. Andriessen. "Educational Technology Research: Computer Aided Learning of Foreign Vocabulary." Educational Technology 21 (1981): 46-53.

Methodologies for instruction in foreign languages and computers.

435. Faircloth, A.H. "Effectiveness of a Computer Assisted Instruction Program for Teaching Consumer Credit to Secondary Home Economics Students." Ph.D. dissertation. University of North Carolina at Greensboro, 1984.

436. Flammer, A. Does Computer Assisted Instruction Reduce Individual Differences? Report No. 6. Stanford, CA:

Stanford University Institute for Mathematical Studies in Social Science, 1976.

Overview of study of computers and individual instructional models.

437. Foell, N.A. "Microcomputers and Vocational Industrial Education: The Industrial Cooperative Education Teacher's Perceptions." Journal of Industrial Teacher Education 22 (1984): 6-13.

Uses of microcomputers and industrial cooperative education with emphasis on work place uses.

438. Fox, A. "Quiz Time in the Classroom: Math Competency Series." Creative Computing 8 (1982): 20-22.

Overview of uses of computers in developing math quizzes.

439. Frankel, S.M. "Evaluating an Instructional System in Mathematics." Paper presented at the National Conference on Technology and Education, Washington, DC, January 1981.

440. Frantz, N.R., Jr. The Development and Field Testing of a Computer Managed Delivery System for Individualizing Instruction in Multioccupational Programs for Vocational Education. University of Delaware: Newark, DE, 1977.

Uses of computers in vocational education program that provides for variety of occupational paradigms.

441. Gershman, J., and E. Sakamoto. "Computer Assisted Remediation and Evaluation: A CAI Project for Ontario Secondary Schools." Educational Technology 21 (1981): 40-43.

Ways computers are used in helping students who need remedial assistance.

442. Gerzanick, R. "Microcomputer Remedial Instruction." Computing Teacher 10 (1982): 50-52.

Uses of computers in tutorial and remedial instruction.

443. Goldstein, I.P., and M.L. Miller. AI Based Personal Learning Environments: Directions for Long Term Research. AI Memo 384. Cambridge, MA: Massachusetts Institute of Technology Artificial Intelligence Laboratory, 1976.

Uses of artificial intelligence programs on personal computers.

444. Grossnickle, D.R. "Profile of Change in Education: A High School Faculty Adopts/Rejects Microcomputers." Educational Technology 22 (1982): 17-19.

Case study of technological adoption of microcomputers in a secondary school.

445. ______, and B.A. Laird. "Profile of Change in Education: A High School Uses Microcomputers." Educational Technology 21 (1981): 7-11.

Case study of a high school using microcomputers and the types of learning and social behaviors that accompanied this technological innovation.

446. Halpern, J.W., and S. Liggett. Computers and Composing: How The New Technologies Are Changing Writing. Studies in Writing and Rhetoric Series. Southern Illinois University Press: Carbondale, IL, 1984.

Ways computers are changing instruction and methodology in writing through the use of word processing programs.

447. Hatfield, L.L. "Instructional Computing in Mathematics Teacher Education." Journal of Research and Development in Education 15 (1982): 30-44.

Uses of computers in preparing mathematics teachers.

448. Hativa, N. "Computer Guided Teaching: An Effective Aid for Group Instruction." Computers and Education 8 (1984): 293-303.

Computers in group instruction and ways to make effective use of them in this situation.

449. Hawkins, R., K. Bosworth, B. Chewning, P.M. Day, and D.H. Gustafson. "Adolescents' Use of Computer Based Health Information: The BARN Project." Children and Micro-

computers: Research on The Newest Medium. Edited by M. Chen and W. Paisley. Beverly Hills, CA: Sage, 1985.

Health education/information network and its effectiveness presented.

450. Henderson, R. "Computer Video Instruction in Mathematics: Field Test of an Interactive Approach." Journal for Research in Mathematics Education 16 (1985): 207-224.

Effectiveness of computer and video as a tool of instruction in mathematics.

451. Henderson, R.W. "Effects of Interactive Video/Computer Instruction on the Performance of Underachieving Students in Mathematics." Paper presented at the annual meeting of the American Educational Research Association, Montreal, April 1983.

452. Henry, L.L. "Computers and Middle School Mathematics." Viewpoints in Teaching and Learning 57 (1981): 46-54.

Ways computers are used in teaching of mathematics in grades 6-12.

453. Henry, M., and D. Kamsett. "The Effects of Computer Aided Instruction on Learning and Attitudes In Economics Principles Courses." Journal of Economic Education 10 (1978): 26-34.

Discussion of computers in college economics classes with implications for secondary schools.

454. Hepburn, M.A. New Information Technology in Social Science Education: Viewpoints from Europe and the United States. Proceedings of the annual conference of the Social Science Education Consortium. ERIC ED 258 902, 1983.

455. Herrmann, A.W. "Using the Computer As Writing Teacher: The Heart of Great Debates." Paper presented at the annual summer conference on The Computer: Extension of the Human Mind II, Eugene, OR, July 1983.

456. Hofstetter, F.T. Fourth Summative Report of the Delaware PLATO Project. University of Delaware: Newark, 1979.

Discussion of uses of PLATO and its effectiveness in terms of instruction.

457. Hollis, J.H. "A Learning Model for Computer Reading Programs." Journal of Special Education Technology 5 (1982): 42-44.

Examines computers used in special education reading program.

458. Holmes, G. "Special Double Issue on Computer Assisted Instruction." Computers and the Humanities 18 (1984): 141-249.

Ways computers are being used in humanities courses. Included are instructional sequences using computers.

459. Hopmeier, G.H. "The Effectiveness of Computerized Coaching for Scholastic Aptitude Tests in Individual and Group Modes." Ph.d. dissertation. Florida State University, 1984.

460. Humphrey, J.E. "A Comparison of How Paced and Unpaced Problems Affect Learning During CAI Math Drills." Ph.D. dissertation. West Virginia University, 1983.

461. Indiana University Center for Innovation in Teaching the Handicapped. Evaluating and Providing Feedback on the Effectiveness of Instruction For Handicapped Children Integrated in Inner-City Secondary Schools. Indiana University: Bloomington, 1983.

Status report on uses of computers with handicapped children.

462. Illinois State Office of Education. DISCOVER: A computer Based Career Guidance and Counselor Administrative Support System. A Final Report. Illinois State Office of Education: Springfield, IL, 1977.

Evaluative report on counselor/guidance system driven through a computer management network.

463. Johnson, W.L. "The Mathematical Laboratory and Computer Assisted Instruction." ERIC ED 258 830, 1985.

464. Johnston, J., R. Luker, and J. Mergendoller. Micros in the Middle School: A Snapshot In 1984. Bloomington, IN: Agency for Instructional Technology, 1984.

How microcomputer technology is being used in classrooms and in administrative settings at the middle school level.

465. Joyce, B. "Organizational Homeostasis and Innovation: Tightening the Loose Couplings." Education and Urban Society 15 (1982): 42-69.

Ways to introduce computer innovations in urban school settings.

466. Kane, J.H. "Computers For Composing." Paper presented at the annual meeting of the American Educational Research Association, Montreal, April 1983.

467. Kantowski, M.G. "The Microcomputer and Instruction in Geometry." Viewpoints in Teaching and Learning 57 (1981): 71-81.

Ways in which computers can be used in teaching of geometry including a discussion of LOGO as a prime resource.

468. Klassen, D.L., R.E. Anderson, T.P. Hansen, and D.C. Johnson. A Study of Computer Use and Literacy in Science Education. Final Report. St. Paul, Minnesota Educational Computing Consortium, 1980.

Effectiveness of computers in science education and computer literacy.

469. Knight, C.W., and G.E. Dunkleberger. "The Influence of Computer Managed Self-Paced Instruction on Science Attitudes of Students." Journal of Research in Science Teaching 14 (1977): 551-555.

Positive attributes of using computers and individual instructional paradigms.

470. Kochinski, V.A. "The Effect of CAI for Remediation on the Self-Concepts, Attitudes and Reading Achievement of Middle School Readers." Ph.D. dissertation. University of Pittsburgh, 1986.

471. Krist, B.J. "Algebra and Instructional Computing." Viewpoints in Teaching and Learning 57 (1981): 55-70.

Ways to teach algebra using computer technology.

472. Kulik, C., B.J. Shwalb, and J.A. Kulik. "Programmed Instruction In Secondary Education: A Meta-Analysis of Evaluation Findings." Journal of Educational Research 75 (1982): 19-26.

Overview of evaluative studies that examined effectiveness of programmed and computer instruction in a variety of secondary school settings.

473. Kulik, J.A. "Effects of Computer Based Teaching on Learners." Paper presented at the National Forum of the College Board Symposium on Computer Competency and Curriculum, Dallas, October 1983.

474. ______, R. Bangert, and G. Williams. "Effects of Computer Based Teaching on Secondary Students." Journal of Educational Psychology 75 (1983): 19-26.

Overview of effectiveness of computer-based teaching in secondary school settings including a discussion of how best to integrate computers within the secondary curriculum.

475. ______, and R.L. Bangert-Drowns. "Effectiveness of Technology in Precollege Mathematics and Science Teaching." Journal of Educational Technology Systems 12 (1984): 137-158.

Discusses questions regarding effectiveness of computer technology in secondary mathematics and science teaching.

476. Kurth, R.J., and L.J. Stromberg. "Using Word Processing in Composition Instruction." Paper presented at the American Reading Forum, Sarasota, FL, December 1984.

477. Laddaga, R. Research on Uses of Audio and Natural Language Processing in Computer Assisted Instruction--Third Year Report. Stanford, CA: Stanford University Institute For Mathematical Studies In Social Science, 1977.

Descriptive research report of uses of natural language processing in CAI.

478. Lai, M.K. "Evaluating a Computer Education Program Qualitatively and Quantitatively." Paper presented at the annual meeting of the American Educational Research Association, New Orleans, April 1984.

479. Lally, M. "Computer Assisted Handwriting Instruction and Visual/Kinesthetic Feedback Processes." Paper presented at the Conference on Research on Retardation and Develomental Disabilities, Gatlinburg, TN, March 1981.

480. Lantz, B.S. "An Intelligent CAI System for Teaching Equation Solving." Journal of Computer Based Instruction 10 (1983): 35-42.

Uses of intelligent CAI system at collegiate level with implication for secondary instruction presented.

481. Lantz, J. State of Art Uses of Computers in Vocational Education. Ohio State Advisory Council for Vocational Education: Columbus, 1984.

482. Larson, A. "The Availability and Use of Computer Instructional Resources in Secondary Education, 1969-1983." Journal of Business Education 60 (1984): 60-62.

Describes ways computers are being used in secondary business education classes.

483. Loftus, G.R., and E.F. Loftus. Mind at Play: The Psychology of Video Games. New York: Basic Books, 1983.

How video games affect thinking and behavior patterns.

484. Lumsden, K.G., and A. Scott. "The Comparative Advantage of Microcomputers in Economics Teaching." Economics 19 (1983): 87-89.

Positive attributes of using microcomputers in the teaching of economics and the implications for secondary education.

485. Maola, J., and G. Kane. "Comparison of Computer Based Versus Counselor Based Occupational Information Systems with Disadvantaged Students." Journal of Counseling Psychology 23 (1976): 163-165.

Differing strategies for providing occupational information to students.

486. Marsh, M.M. "Computer Assisted Learning in the Social Studies: Development and Evaluation of a Series of Computer Programs for Middle School Students." Ph.D. dissertation. University of Maryland, 1984.

487. Mayer, N.P. "A Descriptive Analysis of Computer Education Programs in Texas Secondary Schools and a Proposed Computer Science Program." Ph.D. dissertation. North Texas State University, 1979.

488. McGettick, A.D. "Mathematics by Computer Assisted Learning (CAL)--The Real Problems." International Journal of Mathematical Education in Science and Technology 10 (1979): 65-73.

Problems associated with using computer assisted learning in the mathematics classroom including the lack of effective software.

489. McGrath, D. "Artificial Intelligence. A Tutorial for Educators." Electronic Learning 4 (1984): 39-43.

Overview of artificial intelligence and its possible applications for secondary school situations.

490. McKenzie, J. "A Graphical CAL Program for the Fourier Series." Physics Education 17 (1982): 278-282.

Application of computers and physics at the college level with implications for secondary schools.

491. Merritt, R.L. "Achievement with and without Computer Assisted Instruction in the Middle School." Ph.D. dissertation. University of Southern Mississippi, 1982.

492. Meyer, L.A. "Evaluation Research in Basic Skills with Incarcerated Adults." Paper presented at the annual meeting of the American Educational Research Association, Montreal, April 1983.

493. Modisett, D.M. "Effects of Computer Assisted Instruction on Achievement in Remedial Secondary Mathematical Computation." Ph.D. dissertation. Fordham University, 1980.

494. Moore, J.L. "Development of a Questionnaire to Measure Secondary School Pupils' Attitudes to Computers and Robots." Educational Studies 11 (1985): 33-40.

495. Morrison, J.L. "Project B.E.A.T.: Business Education Alternatives for Teaching." Business Education Forum 32 (1978): 5-6, 9, 11.

Ways computers can be used in business education programs.

496. ______. "Computer Based Instruction Facilities Learning of Basic Business Principles." Business Education Forum 38 (1984): 36-38.

Use of computer technology in beginning business classes.

497. Moser, J.M., and T.P. Carpenter. Using the Microcomputer To Teach Problem Solving Skills: Program Development and Initial Pilot Study (Working Paper No. 328). Madison: University of Wisconsin-Madison, Wisconsin Center for Education Research, 1982.

Development of problem solving skills program using computer technology.

498. Moskowitz, C.M. "Reading Teachers' Reactions to a Field Test of a Computer Assisted Instruction Reading Program in a Microcomputer Laboratory Setting in a Middle School." Ph.D. dissertation. University of Nebraska-Lincoln, 1984.

499. Mullen, F.M. "The Relationship Between Learner Control, Field Orientation, and Achievement in Computer Assisted Instruction on Measurement for Industrial Arts

Students." Ph.D. dissertation. East Texas State University, 1983.

500. Nakhleh, M.B. "An Overview of Microcomputers in Secondary Science Curriculum." Journal of Computers in Mathematics and Science Teaching 31 (1983): 362-368.

Ways computers are being used in math and science instruction.

501. Narita, S. "An Investigation of a Relationship Between Educational Philosophies and Attitudes Toward Computer Managed and Computer Assisted Instruction in Secondary Regular and Special Education Teachers." Ph.D. dissertation. University of Wisconsin-Madison, 1983.

502. Neason, A.B., and W.W. Miller. "The Role of Computers in Vocational Agriculture Instruction." Paper presented at the annual meeting of the American Vocational Association, Washington, DC, December 1982.

503. Noda, P.C. "Exploratory Study of the Impact of Computer Assisted Instruction on the English Language Reading Achievement of LEP Arabic and Chaldean Middle School Students. Ph.D. dissertation. Wayne State University, 1983.

504. Oden, R.E. "An Assessment of the Effectiveness of Computer Assisted Instruction on Altering Teacher Behavior and the Achievement and Attitudes of Ninth Grade Pre-Algebra Students." Ph.D. dissertation. Wayne State University, 1982.

505. Okey, J.R. "The Effectiveness Of Computer Based Education: A Review." Paper presented at the annual meeting of the National Association for Research in Science Teaching, French Lick, IN, April 1985.

506. Oody, G. "Microcomputers for the Gifted: The Pros and Cons." Tennessee Education 14 (1982): 3-11.

Discussion of computers in gifted and talented programs with notes on problems that may arise as a result of their use.

507. Orr, W.T., Jr. "Committed To Computers." Florida Vocational Journal 7 (1982): 8-16.

Computer uses in vocational education instruction.

508. Otts, D. "The Reading Estimate Program: A Computerized Method for Calculating The Raygor Readability Estimate." Computers, Reading and Language Arts 2 (1985): 30-31, 1985.

Use of computers in calculating readability programs.

509. Overton, V. "Research in Instructional Computing and Mathematics Education." Viewpoints in Teaching and Learning 57 (1981): 23-36.

Development of computer mathematical programs and their effectiveness.

510. Palmer, J.T. "Technology, Career Development and Special Needs Students." Career Development for Exceptional Individuals 7 (1984): 3-11.

Use of technology in career education programs for special education students.

511. Pasquino, A., and H.A. Peelle. "Teaching Ecology with a Programming Language." AEDS Journal 9 (1975): 15-26.

Uses of computer langauges in the teaching of ecology.

512. Perkins, D.N. "Educational Heaven: Promises and Perils of Instruction Via Video Games." Video Games and Human Development. Harvard Graduate School of Education: Cambridge, MA, 1983.

Problems of video game instruction as related to computer technology delivery systems.

513. Petosa, R., and T. Gillespie. "Microcomputers in Health Education: Characteristics of Quality Instructional Software." Journal of School Health 54 (1984): 394-396.

Types of software that are useful in health education classrooms.

514. Piel, E.J. "Evaluation of Hunnington II Project on Computer Simulation." Journal of Educational Technology Systems 3 (1975): 303-312.

Computers and simulations are discussed in a positive mode.

515. Porinchak, P.M. "Computer Assisted Instruction in Secondary School Reading: Interaction of Cognitive and Affective Factors." Ph.D. dissertation. Hofstra University, 1983.

516. Powell, J.D., and H.E. Speece. "Computer Awareness Laboratory." Journal of Educational Technology Systems 6 (1978): 45-50.

Development of a laboratory to teach computer literacy and awareness.

517. Pulos, S., and S. Fisher. Socio-Economic Differences In Adolescents' Attitudes Towards Computers. Berkeley, CA: University of California, 1984.

Discussion of perceptions of computer technology using socio/economic differencese as a major variable. Findings indicate that students from a higher socio/economic background have more positive attitudes about computer technology than those with a lower socio/economic status.

518. Rao, A.K., and G.S. Rao. "A Pilot CAI Scheme for the Malaysian Secondary Education System." Journal of Science and Mathematics Education in Southeast Asia 5 (1982): 12-17.

Uses of CAI in a third world country as part of an overall education plan.

519. Rayman, J.R. "The Field Trial of DISCOVER: A New Computerized Interactive Guidance System." Vocational Guidance Quarterly 26 (1978): 349-359.

See item #441.

520. Reed, B.B. "The Effects of Computer-Assisted Instruction on Achievement and Attitudes of Underachievers in High School Biology." Ph.D. dissertation. University of Georgia, 1986.

521. Reed, S.K. "Effect of Computer Graphics on Improving Estimates in Algebra Word Problems." Journal of Educational Psychology 77 (1985): 285-298.

Findings indicate graphic enhancement assists students in learning algebraic functions.

522. Robinson, P. "Computer Literacy of Eighth Grade Students with Implications for Computer Curriculum Development." Ph.D. dissertation. Auburn University, 1985.

523. Rodenstein, J. "Microcomputers in Vocational Education." Electronic Learning 2 (1983): 54-59.

Overview of vocational education computer technology projects and problems.

524. Rodrigues, R.J. "The Computer Based Writing Program from Load to Print." English Journal 73 (1984): 27-30.

Analysis of computer writing project, student reaction, and instructional devices for implementation.

525. Roecks, A.L, and J. Chapin. "Mathematics Achievement in Schools Having and Not Having CMI: An Assessment of MICA E.S.E.A. Title III Computer Managed Instruction Program, MICA Management of Instruction with Computer Assistance." Paper presented at the annual meeting of the American Educational Research Association, New York, April 1977.

526. Roman, R.A. The Word Problem Program: Summative Evaluation. Pittsburgh: University of Pittsburgh, 1975.

Use of word problems and computers as a mechanism in their solution.

527. Romero, S.R. "The Effectiveness of Computer Assisted Mathematics at the Middle School." Ph.D. dissertation. University of the Pacific, 1979.

528. Rosen, A.I. "Computer Analysis of a System of Concurrent Vectors." Physics Teacher 13 (1975): 237-238.

Applications of computers in a physics problem solving situation. Implications for high school classrooms noted.

529. Rosenbaum, N.J. "Problems with Current Research in Writing Using The Microcomputer." Paper presented at the Spring Conference of the Delaware Valley Writing Council and Villanova University's English Department, Villanova, PA, February 1984.

530. Rubincam, I., and W.P. Oliver. "An Investigation of Limited Learner Control Options in a CAI Mathematics Course." AEDS Journal 18 (1985): 11-26.

Ways that learners control a mathematics program in terms of their problem solving options.

531. Sadowski, B. "Research Notes: Critical Thinking and CAI." Journal of Computers in Mathematics and Science Teaching 4 (1985): 12-13.

Ways computers can be used to increase critical thinking skills. Analysis includes notes on effective courseware and teaching methodologies.

532. Samson, G.E., R. Niemiec, T. Weinstein, and H.J. Walberg. "Effects of Computer Based Instruction On Secondary School Achievement: A Quantitative Synthesis." Paper presented at the annual meeting of the American Educational Research Association, Chicago, April 1985.

533. San Antonio State Hospital. Development and Demonstration of the Use of an Integrated Instructional Delivery System for Appliction In Technical/Vocational Education. San Antonio State Hospital: San Antonio, 1984.

Computers and video used in an interactive mode for vocational training in a state hospital school situation.

534. Sarapata, S.L. "The Effective Use of Computers in Township High School District 214." American Annals of the Deaf 128 (1983): 681-684.

Ways computers have been used with hearing impaired secondary students.

535. Savage, E.M. "An Investigation of the Computer Science Educational Opportunities in the Secondary Schools of Maine." Ph.D. dissertation. George Peabody College for Teachers, 1980.

536. Schenk, R., and J. Silvia. "Why Has CAI Not Been More Successful in Economic Education: A Note." Journal of Economic Education 15 (1984): 239-242.

Critical analysis of CAI in economics classes. Implications for secondary social studies classes.

537. Schmidt, L.R. "The Effect of Computer-Assisted Instruction on Reading Achievement and Reading Attitudes of Remedial Junior High School Students." Ph.D. dissertation. Lehigh University, 1986.

538. Searles, J.E. "Information Technology and the Social Studies." Social Education 47 (1983): 335-337.

Ways that computer technology has and will impact on the social studies classroom over the next twenty-five years.

539. Seidel, R.J. D.C. Secondary Schools Project For Adopting Computer Aided Instruction. Human Resources Research Organization, Alexandria, VA, 1978.

Overview of adopt/adapt cycle of technological innovation in a large urban school system.

540. Senthna, G.H. "Development of an Instrument for Evaluation of Micro-Computer Based Simulation Courseware for the High School Physics Classroom." Ph.D. dissertation. University of Houston, 1985.

541. Sharples, M. "The Use of Computers To the Teaching of Creative Writing." AEDS Journal 16 (1983): 79-91.

Using computers in writing and composition including discussion of word processing programs.

542. Shavelson, R., J. Winkler, C. Stasz, W. Feibel, A. Robyn, and S. Shaka. Teaching Mathematics and Science: Patterns of Microcomputer Use. Santa Monica, CA: Rand Corporation, 1984.

Study of ways computers are being used in math and science programs nationwide. Measures of effectiveness of various programs noted.

543. Shaw, E.L., Jr., and J.R. Okey. "Effects of Microcomputer Simulations on Achievement and Attitudes of Middle School Students." Paper presented at the annual meeting of the Association for Research in Science Teaching, French Lick, IN, April 1985.

544. Shinohara, F. "Improvement of Science and Mathematics Education with the Use of Computer Assisted Instruction (CAI) System." Journal of Science and Mathematics Education in Southeast Asia 4 (1981): 42-49.

Ways computers can enhance science and math programs in various Southeast Asian countries.

545. Shostak, R. "Computer Assisted Composition Instruction: Some Promising Practices." Pipeline 8 (1983): 4-6.

Pedagogical implications of using computers in composition classes.

546. Singer, B. "How the Literature and a Research Study Agree on CAI Innovation Success or Failure." School Science and Mathematics 83 (1983): 307-317.

Success of a CAI program measured in terms of literature and research studies.

547. Singer, B.R. "An Investigative Study of Possible Effects of Programming Instruction on Math Anxiety and Teacher Attitudes Toward CAI." Journal of Computers in Mathematics and Science Teaching 5 (1986): 40-43.

Studies on effects of inservice training using computer programming languages to ease teachers' math anxiety levels. Results indicate levels lessened for those using LOGO/PILOT.

548. Soloway, E., K. Ehrlich, J. Bonar, and J. Greenspan. "What Do Novices Know About Programming?" Directions in Human Computer Interaction. Edited by A. Badre and B. Schneiderman. Hillsdale, NJ: Ablex, 1982.

Entry level abilities of students entering programming classes discussed.

549. ______, J. Lockhead, and J. Clement. "Does Computer Programming Enhance Problem Solving Ability? Some

Positive Evidence on Algebra Word Problems." Computer Literacy. Edited by R. Seidel, R. Anderson, and B. Hunter. New York: Academic Press, 1982.

Study ties together computer programming skills and critical thinking skills in solving algebra problems.

550. Stake, B.E. "PLATO and Fourth Grade Mathematics." Paper presented at the annual meeting of the American Educational Research Association, Toronto, March 1978.

551. Stein, J. "Part II: Microcomputer Uses To Promote Physical Proficiency and Motor Development of Students with Handicapped Conditions." Physical Educator 41 (1984): 153-156.

Ways to develop computer uses with physically handicapped children.

552. Stoltman, J.P. "Conference on Computer Assisted Learning in Geography." Journal of Geography 82 (1983): 280-281.

Paper relating ways that computer technology can be used in the teaching of geography.

553. Storm, R.D. "A Model for Implementation of Microcomputer Use into a Program for the Hearing Impaired." American Annals of the Deaf 128 (1983): 535-552.

Model techniques for using microcomputers with deaf children.

554. Summerville, L.J. "The Relationship Between Computer Assisted Instruction and Achievement Levels and Learning Rates of Secondary School Students in First Year Chemistry." Ph.D. dissertation. The American University, 1984.

555. Suydam, M.N. "What Research Says: Microcomputers and Mathematics Instruction." School Science and Mathematics 84 (1984): 337-430.

CAI and CMI uses of computers in the teaching of mathematics.

556. Taylor, J.A., and J.W. Parrish. "A National Survey on The Uses of, and Attitudes Toward, Programmed Instruction and Computers in Public School and College Music Education." _Journal of Computer Based Instruction_ 5 (1978): 11-21.

Research report on status of computer technology in music classes.

557. Texas State Technical Institute. _Exemplary/Innovative. An Application of Computer Graphics Curriculum to Selected Vocational/Technical Programs_. Texas State Technical Institute: Sweetwater, TX, 1984.

Uses of computer graphics in design and vocational education classes are described.

558. Thomas, D.B. "The Effectiveness of Computer Assisted Instruction: Secondary Schools." _AEDS Journal_ 12 (1979): 103-116.

Study on ways CAI can effectively be used in high school classrooms.

559. Thomas, R.A. "Computer Literacy in the High School." _AEDS Journal_ 9 (1976): 71-77.

Overview of computer literacy and problems associated with teaching computer use to high school students.

560. Tindall, L.W., and J.J. Gugerty. "Microcomputers for the Vocational Education of Special Needs Students." Paper presented at the annual meeting of the American Vocational Association, St. Louis, December 1982.

561. Upitis, R. "Milestones in Computer Music Instruction." _Music Educators Journal_ 69 (1983): 32-38.

Effective uses of computers in music education.

562. Vazquez, C.L. "The Effects of Computer Assisted Instruction in Chemistry Science Achievement at the Secondary School Level." Ph.D. dissertation. University of Connecticut, 1983.

563. Versteegh-Limberg, J.E.A. _Computers and Curricula in the New Jersey Secondary Public Schools_. Trenton State College: Trenton, NJ, 1978.

Status report on computer implementation in New Jersey secondary schools.

564. Vincent, A.T. "The Effects Of Supplementary Computer Assisted Instruction on the Mathematics Achievement and Attitude Toward Mathematics of EMR High School Students." Ph.D. dissertation. University of Cincinnati, 1977.

565. Wainwright, C.L. "The Effectiveness of a Computer Assisted Instruction Package in Supplementing Teaching of Selected Concepts in High School Chemistry: Writing Formulas and Balancing Chemical Equations." Ph.D. dissertation. University of Minnesota, 1984.

566. Ware, R.J. "Use of Computer Instruction in Rural Schools to Increase Curriculum Opportunities for the College Bound Student." ERIC ED 231 582, 1983.

567. Watson, R.P. "Computer Based Projects in Science Education: An Overview." _Journal of College Science Teaching_ 12 (1983): 375-380.

Ways computers are used to promote science education. Implications for secondary education noted.

568. Willett, J.B. "A Meta-Analysis of Instructional Systems Applied in Science Teaching." _Journal of Research in Science Teaching_ 20 (1983): 405-417.

Use of computers in science classroom is analyzed as part of a review of methodologies currently being applied in classroom settings.

569. Woodruff, E. "On the Road To Computer Assisted Compositions." _Journal of Eductional Technology Systems_ 10 (1981): 133-148.

Ways to teach writing via computer instruction.

570. Wright, P.A. "A Study of Computer Assisted Instruction for Remediation in Mathematics on the Secondary Level." Ph.D. dissertation. Pepperdine University, 1983.

571. Yuen, C. "An Analysis of Vocational Teachers' Understandings of and Attitudes Toward Using Microcomputers in Vocational Education." ERIC ED 241 744, 1984.

General

572. Adams, C.F. "Project Impact: A Computer Based Student Achievement Information System." Paper presented at the annual meeting of the Americn Educational Research Association, Los Angeles, April 1981.

573. ______, and R. Howland. "The Effects of Student Achievement Information System on Students Learning." Journal of Educational Technology Systems 11 (1982): 215-224.

Study guide systems of CAI/CMI and their effectiveness on learning.

574. Adams, J.A. "Networked Computers Promote Computer Literacy and Computer Assisted Instruction." Technological Horizons in Education 11 (1984): 95-99.

Effects of a computer network environment discussed.

575. Adams, M. "Computer Use in the Portland Public Schools. An Evaluation: Computer Based Instruction, Computer Literacy Programs, Computer Management." ERIC ED 240 158, 1983.

576. Aldinger, L.E. "A Case Study of Curriculum Decision Making in a K-12 Computer Literacy Program." Paper presented at the annual meeting of the American Educational Research Association, Chicago, April 1985.

577. Allen, B.S. "The Effect of System Assigned Exemplar Comparison Strategies On Acquisition Coordinate Concepts." Paper presented at the annual convention of the Association for Educational Communications and Technology, Anaheim, CA, January 1985.

578. Allen, M. "Computer Managed Instruction." Journal of Research and Development in Education 14 (1980): 33-40.

Review of the effectiveness of CMI in several learning situations.

579. Amarel, M. "The Classroom: An Instructional Setting for Teachers, Students and the Computer." Classroom Computers and Cognitive Science. Edited by A.C. Wilkinson. New York: Academic Press, 1983.

Environmental effects of the introduction of computers in a classroom situation.

580. ______. "The Introduction of Innovative Instructional Systems: Implementation and Program Evaluation. Section I. The Practitioner Selection, Training, and Program Evaluation: Section 2. Degree of Implementation and Classroom Observation." Paper presented at the annual meeting of the American Educational Research Association, Washington, DC, April 1975.

581. Anandam, K., and J.T. Kelly. "Evaluating the Use of Technology in Education." Paper presented at the National Conference on Technology and Education, Washington, DC, January 1981.

582. Anderson, D.O. "Microcomputers in Education." Journal of Learning Disabilities 15 (1982): 368-369.

Ways microcomputers are being used with learning disabled students.

583. ______, and D.J. Glowinski. "Effective Use of Computer Managed Instruction Program." Journal of Learning Disabilities 15 (1982): 555-556.

Analyzes reward-reinforcement structure of CMI programs with the learning disabled.

584. Anderson, R. "The Affective and Cognitive Effects of Microcomputer Based Science Instruction." Journal of Educational Technology Systems 9 (1980): 329-355.

Description of overall effects of computers in science instruction.

585. ______, D.L. Klassen, K.R. Krohn, and P. Smith-Cunnien. Computer Awareness and Literacy: An Empirical Assess-

ment. Minneapolis: Minnesota Educational Computing Consortium, 1982.

Analyzes assessment of large-scale computer literacy programs in the State of Minnesota.

586. ______, W.W. Welch, and L.J. Harris. "Inequities in Opportunities for Computer Literacy." The Computing Teacher 11 (1984): 10-12.

Differences in school environments as measured by socio/economic differences and ability to become computer literate discussed.

587. Andrews, J., and J. Strain. "Computer Assisted Distance Education: Off-Line and On-Line American Experiences." Distance Education 6 (1985): 143-157.

Use of computer in providing education away from single-classroom situations.

588. Ash, R.C. "An Analysis of the Cost Effectiveness of a Computer Assisted Instructional Program." Ph.d. dissertation. Auburn University, 1985.

589. Association for the Development of Computer Based Instructional systems. Mission of the Future. Volume I and II. Association for the Development of Computer Based Instructional Systems: Bellingham, WA, 1979.

Papers from the Association of Computer Instructional Systems.

590. Computer Based Instruction: A New Decade. Association for the Development of Computer Based Instructional Systems: Bellingham, WA, 1980.

See item #589.

591. Atwood, M.E., and H.R. Ramsey. Cognitive Structures in the Comprehension and Memory of Computer Debugging. Alexandria, VA: U.S. Army Research Institute for the Behavioral and Social Sciences, 1978.

592. Ayers, G.E. "The Learner and the Computer." Paper presented at the National Conference on Computer Based Education, Bloomington, MN, October 1980.

593. Badre, A., and B. Schneiderman. Directions in Human Computer Interaction. Norwood, NJ: Ablex, 1982.

Ways computers and computer systems may be used in the future including a discussion of intelligent learning systems.

594. Baird, W. "Conference Abstracts: Microcomputers in Education." Journal of Computers in Mathematics and Science Teaching 4 (1985): 51-52.

Papers on uses of computers in mathematics and science instruction.

595. Baker, F.B. Computer Managed Instruction: Theory and Practice. Englewood Cliffs, NJ: Educational Technology Publishers, 1978.

Text on developing CMI instructional sequences.

596. Bardige, A. "The Problem Solving Revolution." Classroom Computer News 3 (1983): 44-46.

Discussion of ways computers can be used to develop problem-solving skills.

597. Barnhardt, R., and C. Barnhardt. "Chipping Away at Rural School Problems: The Alaskan Experience with Educational Technology." Phi Delta Kappan 65 (1983): 274-278.

Ways computers are used in Alaska to solve distance and teacher shortage problems.

598. Barr, A., M. Beard, and R.C. Atkinson. The Computer As a Tutorial Laboratory: The Stanford BIP Project. Stanford, CA: Stanford University Institute for Mathematical Studies in the Social Sciences, 1975.

Computer as a tutor in a variety of situations.

599. Bates, M., and K. Wilson. ILIAD: Interactive Instruction Assistance for the Deaf. Bolt, Beranek, and Newman, Inc.: Cambridge, MA, 1981.

Uses of computer technology in an interaction voice-activated mode.

600. Baughman, S.S., and P.D. Clagett. <u>Video Games and Human Development: Research Agenda for the '80s</u>. Cambridge, MA: Harvard University Graduate School of Education, 1983.

Research questions involving effects of video games on human psyche analyzed.

601. Beal, J.L. <u>State of Washington Computer Use Survey</u>. University of Washington: Seattle, WA, 1983.

Uses of computer technology in Washington State.

602. Beck, J.J., Jr. "Analysis of Student Attitude Toward Computer Assisted Instruction in Nebraska Public High Schools." Ph.D. dissertation. Univerity of Nebraska at Lincoln, 1979.

603. Becker, H.J. <u>Microcomputers in the Classroom--Dreams and Realities</u>. Johns Hopkins University Center for Social Organization of Schools: Baltimore, MD, 1982.

Status of computer usage in classrooms and schools throughout the United States.

604. _____. "How Schools Use Microcomputers." <u>Classroom Computer Learning</u> 12 (1983): 41-44.

See item #603.

605. _____. <u>School Uses Of Microcomputers</u> (Issue 1). Baltimore, MD: The Johns Hopkins Center for Social Organization of Schools, 1983.

Studies on computer usage including who are using them, effectiveness in instruction, types of programs being used, socioeconomic differences, and use by male and female students.

606. _____. <u>School Uses of Microcomputers</u> (Issue 2). Baltimore, MD: The Johns Hopkins Center for Social Organization of Schools, 1983.

607. _____. <u>School Uses of Microcomputers</u> (Issue 3). Baltimore, MD: The Johns Hopkins Center for Social Organization of Schools, 1983.

608. ______. School Uses of Microcomputers (Issue 4). Baltimore, MD: The Johns Hopkins Center for Social Organization of Schools, 1984.

609. ______. "Computers in Schools Today: Some Basic Considerations." American Journal of Education 93 (1984): 22-39.

610. ______. "The Social Context of Using Computers in Schools: It's Not Just a Matter of Good Software." Paper presented at the Workshop On Computer Literacy, Paris, June 1984.

611. ______. "How Schools Use Microcomputers: Results from a National Survey." Children and Microcomputers: Research on the Newest Medium. Edited by M. Chen and W. Paisley. Beverly Hills, CA: Sage, 1985.

612. ______. "Men and Women As Computer Using Teachers." Sex Roles 13 (1985): 137-148.

Status of how computers are used in schools by gender.

613. ______. "School Uses of Computers: Results of the Second Survey." Paper presented at the Educational Testing Service Sociology Seminar, Princeton, NJ, 1985.

614. Behrmann, M.M., and L. Lahm. Proceedings of the National Conference on the Use of Microcomputers in Social Education. The Council for Exceptional Children: Reston, VA, 1984.

615. Bell, F.H. "Computer Literacy, School Mathematics and Problem Solving: Three for the Price of One." AEDS Journal 12 (1979): 163-170.

Ways computers are used in mathematics and problem-solving situations.

616. Berg, R. "Analytical Criteria for Microcomputer Based Simulation/Games." Paper presented at the annual conference of the Social Science Education Consortium, Athens, GA, June 1983.

617. Bergman, S., and Y. Varol. "Helping the Teacher Teach in Israel: A Computer Experiment." Educational Technology 16 (1976): 48-51.

Uses of computers in Israeli schools.

618. Bertram, B. "Reviewing the Black History Show: How Computers Can Change the Writing Process." ERIC ED 247 544, 1984.

619. Bialo, E.R., and L.B. Erickson. "Microcomputer Courseware: Characteristics and Design Trends." Paper presented at the annual meeting of the American Educational Research Association, New Orleans, April 1984.

620. Billings, K. "Computer Assisted Learning: A Learner Driven Model." Paper presented at the Summer Conference on the Computer: The Extension of the Human Mind, Eugene, OR, July 1982.

621. Bingham, M., and J.J. Manock. "Providing Assistance for the Implementation of Educational Micrcomputers--A Statewide Approach." Technological Horizons in Education 9 (1982): 101-105.

Difference in computer implementation on a state by state basis.

622. Bitter, G.G. "Survey of Arizona Public School Practices and Needs for Computer Assisted Instruction." ERIC ED 218 704, 1980.

623. _____. "Microcomputers and Problem Solving." ERIC ED ED 218 705, 1981.

624. Blaschke, C.L. "Technology Trends in Special Education." Technological Horizons in Education 12 (1985): 73-77.

Ways computers are being used in a variety of special education situations including the physically disabled.

625. Boileau, D.M. "Programmed Instruction: A Lull Before The Storm." Communication Education 32 (1983): 137-143.

Overview of programmed instruction and hypothesis that it will need to be reviewed if computer instruction is to be effective.

626. Bollerslev, P., and N. Estes. "Changes In Curricula and Institutional Structures." Paper presented at the International Conference on Education and New Information Technologies, Paris, July 1984.

627. Bolter, J.D. *Turing's Man - Western Culture in the Computer Age*. Chapel Hill, NC: The University of North Carolina Press, 1984.

History of technology and its effects on Western culture and civilization.

628. Bolton, H., and D.K. Moscow. "Microcomputers in the Classroom: A Foot in the Door." *Educational Computer Magazine* 1 (1981): 34-36.

Curricular areas in which microcomputers are being used in school situations.

629. Borg, K. "Computer Teaching in Sweden." *Technological Horizons In Education* 8 (1981): 41-42.

Overview of uses of computer technology in Swedish schools.

630. Bork, A. "Learning To Teach Via Teaching the Computer To Teach." *Journal of Computer Based Instruction* 2 (1975): 76-96.

Using programming as part of instruction.

631. ______. "Computers In Education Today--and Some Possible Futures." *Phi Delta Kappan* 66 (1984): 239-243.

Status of computers in schools and a positive scenario of integrating computers in schools in the future.

632. ______, and S.D. Franklin. "The Role Of Personal Computer Systems in Education." *AEDS Journal* 13 (1979): 17-30.

How computers can be used to improve schooling.

633. Boyd, G.M. "Learner Support Options in Computer Assisted Learning." Computers and Education 8 (1984): 349-354.

Different ways computers might be used in educational environments.

634. Bracey, G.W. "Computers in Education: What the Research Shows." Electronic Learning 2 (1982): 51-54.

Overview of research studies showing computer effectiveness.

635. Bradley, C. "Information Processing Styles, Computer Programming and Achievement." Journal of Educational Computer Research 1 (1985): 427-433.

How different learning styles are and are not adaptable to computer instruction.

636. Brawer, J. "The Effectiveness of the Computer and Television in Teaching Basic Relational Concepts: A Comparative Study." Paper presented at the annual meeting of the International Communication Association, San Francisco, July 1984.

637. Bright, G.W. "Explaining the Efficiency of Computer Assisted Instruction." AEDS Journal 16 (1983): 144-152.

Why computers effect certain learning situations.

638. Brown, A. A Practical Approach to Computer Based Instructional Support. Alberta Department of Education: Edmonton, Alberta, 1980.

Implementation of computer education through an integrated instructional approach.

639. Brown, D.U. "An Investigation into the Current Attitudes and Perceptions Held by Educators Toward Computer Assisted Instruction." Ph.D. dissertation. The University of Iowa, 1981.

640. Brown, J.S. "Steps Toward a Theoretical Foundation for Complex, Knowledge Based CAI." ERIC ED 135 365, 1975.

641. Brunken, P. "Independence for the Visually Handicapped Through Technology." Education of the Visually Handicapped 15 (1984): 127-133.

Uses of computers with the visually blind and handicapped.

642. Bruwelheide, J.H. "A Needs Assessment To Determine Computer Literacy Goals in Montana." Ph.D. dissertation. Utah State University, 1983.

643. Brzezinski, E. "Microcomputers and Testing: Where Are We and How Did We Get There?" Educational Measurement: Issues and Practice 3 (1984): 7-10.

Issues in using microcomputers as part of evaluation systems.

644. Bunderson, C.V., and G.W. Faust. "Programmed and Computer Assisted Instruction." The Psychology of Teaching Methods: The Seventy-Fifth Yearbook of the National Society for the Study of Education (Part I). Edited by N.L. Gage. Chicago: University of Chicago Press, 1976.

Overview of ties between programmed instructional techniques and CAI.

645. Burley, R.C. "LRPSI Staff Development Activities." ERIC ED 255 743, 1985.

646. Burns, H. "The Brainbrow Connection: Supplementing the Romance of Classroom Color Computing." Pipeline 7 (1982): 4-6.

Use of color printing and graphics in schools.

647. Burns, M.B., and L. Swearingen. "A Justification for the Use of Computer Assisted Instruction for the Physically Handicapped." Paper presented at the Council for Exceptional Children's National Conference on the Use Of Microcomputers In Special Education, March 1983.

648. Burton, R.R., and J.S. Brown. "A Tutoring and Modeling Paradigm for Gaming Environments." SIGCSE Bulletin 8 (1976): 236-246.

Ways to develop models for games and tutoring programs.

649. Caldwell, R.M. "Improving Learning Strategies with Computer Based Education." Theory into Practice 19 (1980): 141-143.

Ways to improve teaching techniques via the incorporation of computers in the classroom.

650. Calfee, R. "Computer Literacy and Book Literacy: Parallels and Contrasts." Educational Researcher 14 (1985): 8-13.

Need to become totally literate via books and technology discussed and debated.

651. Calkins, A. "EL's First Annual Survey on State Governments and the New Technologies." Electronic Learning 1 (1981): 56-59, 84.

Ways information technology is being implemented in state governments.

652. Campbell, L.P. "On the Horizon: A Computer in Every Classroom." Education 104 (1984): 332-334.

Future of computers in schools and the ways they may be used.

653. Campbell, P.B. "Computers in Education. A Question of Access. Access to Computers." Paper presented at the annual meeting of the American Educational Research Association, Montreal, April 1983.

654. Card, S.K., T.P. Moran, and A. Newell. "Computer Text Editing: An Information Processing Analysis of a Routine Cognitive Skill." Cognitive Psychology 12 (1980): 32-34.

How information is processed while editing via a computer is analyzed.

655. Carl, D.L., and S. Hoelscher. "Administrators' Perceptions of Computer Use in Education." Paper presented at the annual meeting of the Association for Educational Communications and Technology, Dallas, January 1984.

656. Carnine, D. "Mainstreaming Computers." Educational Leadership 41 (1984): 77-82.

Use of computers in special education situations that are assisting students who are mainstreamed into regular classes.

657. Carter, J.W. "Feedback Effectiveness via Computer Assisted Video Instruction on the Learning Performance of Handicapped Adolescents." Ph.D. dissertation. University of Oregon, 1984.

658. Cartwright, G.P., and J.L. Dervensky. "An Attitudinal Research Study of Computer Assisted Testing As a Learning Method." Psychology in the Schools 13 (1976): 317-321.

Students surveyed to determine if they like computers as part of their evaluation process. Most prefer using computers.

659. ______. "Computer Applications in Special Education." Instructional Software: Principles and Perspectives for Design and Use. Edited by D.F. Walker and R.D. Hess. Belmont, CA: Wadsworth, 1984.

Types of courseware that have been successful in special education classes.

660. Chandler, H.N. "Skinner and CAI." Journal of Learning Disabilities 17 (1984): 441-442.

Background of CAI and Skinnerian philosophy as related to it.

661. Charp, S. "Effectiveness of Computers in Instruction." Viewpoints in Teaching and Learning 57 (1981): 13-22.

Status of computer television in a variety of curriculum context.

662. _____, and R.N. Sebastian. "Cost Effective Considerations in the Use of a Combined CAI/CMI System." Technological Horizons in Education 5 (1978): 42-46.

How to make computer instruction cost effective.

663. Chambers, J.A., and J.W. Sprecher. "Computer Assisted Instruction: Current Trends and Critical Issues." Communications of the ACM 23 (1980): 332-342.

664. Chapin, J.D. "An Interactive Management Information System for the Support of Individualized Instruction: A Lesson on How To Manage Computer Managed Instruction." Paper presented at the annual meeting of the Americn Educational Research Association, Washington, DC, March 1975.

665. Chen, M. Gender Differences in Computer Uses and Attitudes: A Survey of Five Bay Area High School. Stanford: Stanford University Institute for Communication Research, 1984.

Ways male and female students use computers in school situations.

666. Cimochowski, A.M. "Teacher Preparation in Computer Education: A Follow-Up Survey of American Association of Colleges for Teacher Education Member Institutions." Ph.D. dissertation. University of Connecticut, 1984.

667. Clark, R.E. "Reconsidering Research on Learning From The Media." Review of Educational Research 53 (1983): 445-460.

Analyzes different types of media, including computers, and the research on their effectiveness as learning tools.

668. _____. "Research on Student Thought Processes During Computer Based Instruction." Journal of Instructional Development 7 (1984): 2-5.

What students think about as they're using computer technology.

669. ______. "Learning from Computers: Theoretical Problems." Paper presented at the annual meeting of the American Educational Research Association, New Orleans, April 1984.

670. ______. "Confounding in Educational Computer Research." *Journal of Educational Computing Research* 1 (1985).

Discusses differences in various studies surrounding the effectiveness of CAI and computers in education.

671. ______, and S. Gavriel. "Media in Teaching." *Handbook of Research on Teaching-Third Edition*. Edited by Merlin C. Wittrock. New York: Macmillan, 1986.

672. ______, and R.E. Snow. "Alternative Designs for Instructional Technology Research." *AV Communication Review* 23 (1975): 373-394.

Ways to study the role of media in learning situations; computers included.

673. Clements, F.J. "Affective Considerations in Computer Based Education." *Educational Technology* 21 (1981): 28-32.

How computers affect the affective domains in education.

674. Cline, H.F., R.E. Bennett, R.C. Kershaw, M.B. Schneiderman, B. Steche, and S. Wilson. *The Electronic Schoolhouse: The IBM Secondary School Computer Education Program*. Hillsdale, NJ: Lawrence Erlbaum, 1986.

675. Cohen, V.B. "What Is Instructionally Effective Microcomputer Software?" *Viewpoints in Teaching and Learning* 59 (1983): 13-27.

Evaluation of computer courseware in terms of instructional applications.

676. Coleman, D.P. "Manipulating Causal Attributions to Maximize Students Performance in Math Computer Assisted Instruction." Ph.D. dissertation. University of San Francisco, 1986.

677. Collins, A., J. Passafiume, L. Gould, and J. Carbonell. Improving Interactive Capabilities in Computer Assisted Instruction. Cambridge, MA: Bolt, Beranek, & Newman, Inc., 1973.

Discussion of interactive uses of computer instruction.

678. Collins, E.A., and D.C. Larsen. "Computer Support for a Systems Approach to Instruction: Problem Statement, Data Entry and Group Formation." Journal of Educational Technology Systems 5 (1977): 3-14.

Analyzes systematic instruction via analogies to computer programming.

679. ______. "Computer Support for a Systems Approach To Instruction: Problem Statement and Data Entry Techniques." Paper presented to the annual conference of the Association For Educational Data Systems, Phoenix, May 1976.

680. Collins, S. Computer Technology and Instruction Handbook: Resources. Washington State Office of the State Superintendent of Public Instruction: Olympia, WA, 1983.

Computer resource handbook for Washington State.

681. Congress of the United States. Information Technology in Education. U.S. Government Printing Office: Washington, DC, 1980.

Overview of computer and information technology in public schools throughout the United States. Includes data on implementation, types of computers that have been purchased, and case studies of computers in school situations.

682. Craft, C.O. "Research on the Use of Computer Assisted Instruction." Man/Society/Technology 41 (1982): 26-27.

Ways CAI is being used in a variety of instructional environments.

683. Crealock, C.M. "Creative Writing Competency: A Comparison of Paper and Pencil and Computer Technologies To Improve The Writing Skills of Mildly Handicapped Adolescents." Paper presented at the annual meeting of the American Educational Research Association, Chicago, April 1985.

684. Crist, M. "Computer Education from a Humanistic Perspective." Computers in the Schools 1 (1984): 59-65.

A socio-humanist overview of computers in schools and their effects.

685. Crist-Whitzel, J.L., S.J. Dasho, and L.C. Beckum. Achieving Equity: Student Led Computer Training. San Francisco: Far West Laboratory for Educational Research and Development, 1984.

Students using computers in tutorial situations.

686. Cronbach, L.J., and R.E. Snow. Aptitudes and Instructional Methods: A Handbook for Research on Interactions. New York: Irvington, 1977.

Effectiveness of instructional techniques including computer usage discussed.

687. Crowner, T.T. "Exceptional Children and Microcomputers, A Survey of Public School Applications." Paper presented at the National Conference and Training Workshops on Technology in Special Education, Reno, NV, January 1984.

688. Dalbey, J., and M.C. Linn. Cognitive Consequences of Programming Instruction: Augmenting Instruction in BASIC. Berkeley: University of California, Lawrence Hall of Science, 1984.

How computers affect thinking skills, especially in learning a programming language.

689. Dale, E.J. "A LOGO Physics Project." ERIC ED 254 4200, 1984.

690. Damarin, S.K. "Technology in the Classroom: Initiative Or Response? New Directions In Curriculum Development." Paper presented at the annual meeting of the

American Association of Colleges for Teacher Education, Houston, February 1982.

691. Dammeyer, J.W. "Computer Assisted Learning--Or Financial Disaster." *Educational Leadership* 40 (1983): 7-9.

Discusses cost effectiveness of CAI in school situations.

692. Danziger, J., W.H. Dutton, R. Kling, and K. Kraemer. *Computers and Politics*. New York: Columbia University Press, 1981.

693. Dasho, S.J., and L.C. Beckum. "Microcomputers and Educational Equity: The Promise and Peril." Paper presented at the annual meeting of the American Educational Research Association, Montreal, April 1983.

694. Davy, J. "Mindstorms in the Lamplight." *Teachers College Record* 85 (1984): 549-558.

Discussion of computers and their effects on schools.

695. Dede, C. "The Likely Evolution of Computer Use in Schools." *Educational Leadership* 41 (1983): 22-24.

Ways computers will be used in school environments in the future.

696. Dence, M. "Toward Defining the Role of CAI: A Review." *Educational Technology* 20 (1980): 50-54.

How CAI can be used in current school situations and how it might be used in the future.

697. Department of Education. "Teachers' Views on Computer Use in Elementary and Secondary Schools." Washington, DC: Office of Education Research and Improvement, 1986.

698. Deringer, D.K. "The New Federalism: A Do-It-Yourself Approach to Computers in Education." *Technological Horizons in Education* 9 (1982): 90-94.

Declining role of federal influence in schools and its effect on providing technology in the classrooms.

699. _____. "New Directions for Education?" Educational Leadership 41 (1983): 25.

Discusses computers and their role in education.

700. Dickson, W.P. "Thought-Provoking Software: Juxtaposing Symbol Systems." Educational Researcher 14 (1985): 30-38.

Overview of effective software and description of evaluative tools used to determine its effectiveness.

701. Dickinson, W.P., V.A. Neal, and M.G. Gillingham. "A Low Cost Multimedia Microcomputer System for Educational Research and Development." Educational Technology 23 (1984): 20-22.

702. Diem, R.A. "Computers in a School Environment: Preliminary Report of the Social Consequences." Theory and Research In Social Education 14 (1986): 163-170.

703. _____. "Microcomputer Technology in Educational Environments: Three Case Studies." Journal of Educational Research 80 (1986): 93-98.

704. Douglas, E., and D. Bryant. "Implementing Computer Assisted Instruction: The Garland Way." Technological Horizons in Education 13 (1985): 86-91.

Analyzes use of PLATO/WICAT interactive computer system in a school environment.

705. Dover, A. "Computers and the Gifted: Past, Present, and The Future." Gifted Child Quarterly 27 (1983): 81-85.

Ways computers are used in the gifted classroom.

706. Dunkleberger, G.E., and R.W. Smith. "A Computer Managed Approach to Individualized Instruction." Journal of Chemical Education 53 (1976): 649-650.

How computers can be used in individualized instructional patterns.

707. Earl, G.J. "The Effect of Computer Education on Teacher Use of Microcomputers in The Classroom and Teacher

Perceptions of Potential Use." Ph.D. dissertation. Ball State University, 1984.

708. Eastman, S.T., and K.A. Krendl. "Computers and Gender: Differential Effects of Electronic Speech on Students' Achievement and Attitudes." Paper presented at the Communication, Language and Gender Conference, Miami University, Oxford, May 1984.

709. Edeburn, C.E., and C. Jacobi. "Computer Assisted Instruction for Native American Students." Paper presented at the annual conference of the Northern Rocky Mountain Educational Research Association, Jackson Hole, WY, October 1984.

710. Education Research Service. School District Uses of Computer Technology. Education Research Services: Arlington, VA, 1982.

Status of computer usage in public schools nationwide.

711. Education Turnkey Systems, Inc. Uses of Computers in Education. Education Turnkey Systems: Falls Church, VA, 1985.

See item #710, an update of same.

712. Educational Testing Service. "Computers Are Fun, but Can They Teach?" Educational Testing Service Report 25 (1979).

Reports on the effectiveness of computers as part of instruction.

713. Edwards, J. "Computer Assisted Testing." Journal of Research and Development in Education 14 (1980): 9-15.

Describes use of computers as part of ongoing evaluative sequences.

714. ______, S. Norton, S. Taylor, M. Weiss, and R. Dusseldrop. "How Effective Is CAI? A Review of the Research." Educational Leadership 33 (1975): 147-153.

Early review of CAI research. Emphasis on individual instruction patterns.

715. Edwards, L. "Teaching Higher Level Thinking Skills Through Computer Courseware." <u>AEDS Monitor</u> 21 (1983): 28-30.

Analyzes types of software that promote higher thinking skills.

716. ______. "Teaching Higher Level Thinking Skills Through Computer Courseware." Paper presented at the Council for Exceptional Children National Conference on the Use of Microcomputers In Special Education, Hartford, CT, March 1983.

717. Eisele, J.E. "A Case for Computers in Instruction." <u>Journal of Research and Development in Education</u> 14 (1980): 1-8.

Discusses reasons why computers should be used as part of instructional sequences.

718. Ellis, J.A. "A Comparative Evaluation of Computer Managed Instruction and Instructor Managed Instruction." <u>Proceedings of the Association for the Development of Computer Based Instructional Systems</u>. Bellingham, WA: Association for the Development of Computer Based Instructional Systems, 1978.

Papers analyzing how computers are used as part of a variety of instructional techniques.

719. Emmett, A. "American Education: The Dead End of the 80s." <u>Personal Computing</u> 7 (1983): 96-101, 103, 105.

Laments nonuse of computers in schools.

720. Enell, N.C. "Present and Future Applications in Special Education Research, Evaluation and Planning." Paper presented at the annual meeting of the American Educational Research Association, Montreal, April 1983.

721. ______. "A Cost Comparison of Preparing Special Education Individualized Education Programs (IEPs) with and Without Computer Assistance." Paper presented at the annual meeting of the American Educational Research Association, New Orleans, April 1984.

722. Evans, C. The Micromillenium. New York: Washington Square Publishing Co., 1981.

Classic work on how computers and computer technology could change schools and society as a whole.

723. Fancher, E.P. "Educational Technology: A Black Perspective." ERIC ED 240 213, 1983.

724. Federal Interagency Committee on Education. Teacher Training in the Use of Educational Technology. Washington, DC: Department of Health, Education and Welfare, 1978.

Ways teachers are prepared to use and implement computer technology.

725. Felter, M. "Sex Differences on the California Statewide Assessment of Computer Literacy." Sex Roles 13 (1985): 181-192.

726. Feurzeig, W. Microcomputers in Education. Cambridge, MA: Bolt, Beranek, and Newman, 1981.

Overview of current role of computers in education.

727. Fisher, F.D. "Computer Assisted Education: What's Not Happening?" Journal of Computer Based Instruction 9 (1982): 19-27.

Reasons why computers are not being accepted in large numbers in school situations.

728. Fithugh, R.J. "Computer System Requirements for CAI/CMI Research." Paper presented at the annual meeting of the American Educational Research Association, Toronto, March 1978.

729. Fleming, M.L., and H. Levie. Instructional Message Design. Englewood Cliffs, NJ: Educational Technology Publications, 1978.

Ways to design effective instructional sequences with applications for computer technology.

730. Floria-Ruane, S., and S. Dunn. Teaching Writing: Some Perennial Questions and Some Possible Answers. East Lansing, MI: Michigan State University, 1985.

Computers and word processing programs used to teach writing.

731. Follettie, J.F. Achieving Information in Schools (AIMS): Larger Straws in the Winds of Change. Southwest Regional Laboratory For Educational Research and Development: Los Alamitos, CA: 1976.

Project using computer technology as instrument to monitor achievement gain scores in schools.

732. Forman, D. Instructional Use of Microcomputers: A Report on B.C.'s Pilot Project. British Columbia Department of Education: Victoria, British Columbia, 1981.

733. ______. "Search of the Literature." The Computing Teacher 8 (1982): 37-51.

Overview of research on computer education including CAI and CMI.

734. Foster, C. "An Analysis of the Rise and Fall of Programmed Instruction. Implications For Computer Assisted Instruction." Journal of Special Education Technology 6 (1983): 50-57.

History of programmed instruction, why it failed and the possible pitfalls for computer-based instruction if it follows the same patterns.

735. Frank, A.R. "Teaching Selected Microcomputer Skills to Retarded Students Via Picture Prompts." Journal of Applied Behavior Analysis 18 (1985): 179-185.

Use of computers and computer graphics to teach the learning disabled.

736. Fuchs, L. "Data Based Program Modification: A Continuous Evaluation System with Computer Software to Facilitate Implementation." Journal of Special Education Technology 6 (1983): 50-57.

737. Fullan, M., and A. Pomfret. "Research on Curriculum and Instruction Implementation." Review of Educational Research 47 (1977): 335-397.

Using computers in various instructional modes. Viability of technology in classrooms discussed.

738. Gabel, L.T. "The Impact of a Research Based Model for Inservicing Teachers on Integrating Computer Education into an Elementary Curriculum." Ph.D. dissertation. University of Oregon, 1984.

739. Gagne, R.M. "Instructional Technology: The Research Field." Journal of Instructional Development 8 (1986): 7-14.

740. Galvis, A.H. "A Systematic Model for the Assessment of Teachers' Training Needs in Computer Based Education." Ph.D. dissertation. Pennsylvania State University, 1984.

741. Gambrell, J.B., and R.E. Sandfield. "Computers in the School: Too Much Too Soon?" High School Journal 62 (1979): 327-331.

Discussion of rapid implementation of computer technology without research to back up ideas.

742. Gaushell, H. "Microcomputers in Education." ERIC ED 225 540, 1982.

743. Gilchrist, R., and H.A. Sanders. Implementing Computer Technology In School Systems. Alberta Department of Education: Edmonton, Alberta, 1983.

Ways computers are used in school settings in Alberta, Canada.

744. Goddard, W.P., and B. Hicks. Applications of Computers in the Whole School--Five Examples. Illinois Series On Educational Applications of Computers. State of Illinois Department of Education: Springfield, IL, 1975.

Case studies of computer applications in a variety of educational settings.

745. Goldenberg, E.P. Special Technology for Special Children. Baltimore: University Park Press, 1980.

Ways technology is being used to aid special education students.

746. Goldstein, I.P., and M.L. Miller. AI Based Personal Learning Environments: Directions for Long Term Research. Cambridge, MA: Massachusetts Institute of Technology, Artificial Intelligence Laboratory, 1976.

Artificial intelligence applications for schools. Analyzes areas of future research.

747. Goldstein, I., and S. Papert. "Artificial Intelligence, Language and the Study of Knowledge." Cognitive Science 1 (1977): 84-123.

Overview of artificial intelligence research and its applications to the ways in which the langauge process is developed.

748. Goor, J. Student Use of Computers In Schools. Fall, 1980: A Survey Of Public School Districts. Rockville, MD: Westat Research Inc., 1981.

Status research report on how students are using microcomputers and the subjects most likely to encourage computer utilization.

749. ______. Student Use of Computers in Schools. Washington, DC: National Center For Education Statistics, 1982.

Statistical overview of computer utilization in schools throughout the United States.

750. Grabe, M. "Evaluating the Educational Value Of Microcomputers." Computers in the Schools 1 (1984): 35-44.

Discusses usefulness of computers in schools.

751. Grayson, L. "An Overview of Computers in U.S. Education." Technological Horizons in Education 12 (1984): 78-83.

How and where computers are being used in a variety of educational environments.

752. Green, J.O. "B.F. Skinner's Technology of Teaching." Classroom Computer Learning 4 (1984): 22-29.

Applications of Skinnerian learning principles to computer based instruction.

753. Greenfield, P. Mind and Media: The Effects of Television, Video Games and Computers. Cambridge, MA: Harvard University Press, 1984.

How computers and other forms of media affect cognitive development.

754. Griswold, P.A. "An Evaluation of Bloom's Theory of School Learning in a Computer Assisted Instruction Curriculum." Ph.D. dissertation. Rutgers University, The State University of New Jersey, 1981.

755. ______. Longitudinal Patterns of Students' Attitudes in a Computer Assisted Instruction Curriculum. Denver, CO: Rocky Mountain Educational Research Association, 1981.

Research on how attitudes about computers can change over a period of time.

756. Gummersheimer, V.H. "When Do I Get To Use the Computer?" Computing Teacher 1 (1982): 24-25.

Analyzes availability of computers in classroom situations.

757. Hanley, T. "CAI in Special Education: Research Directions." Peabody Journal of Education 62 (1984): 22-39.

Describes possibilities of research studies involving computer technology and special education, their needs, and implications for special education.

758. Hanley, T.V. Microcomputers in Special Education: Organizational Issues. COSMOS Corporation: Washington, DC, 1983.

Describes ways in which computers are being used in special education classrooms and how they are administratively organized.

759. _____. <u>Microcomputer Software in Special Education: Selection and Management</u>. COSMOS Corporation: Washington, DC, 1983.

Presents evaluation schemas for selecting software for use in special education classrooms.

760. Hargan, C., and B. Hunter. <u>Instructional Computing: Ten Case Studies</u>. Human Resources Research Organization: Alexandria, VA, 1978.

Use of computers in a variety of classroom and educational settings. Discusses and analyzes similarities, differences, and problems.

761. Harris, D., and B. Collison. <u>Proceedings of NECC/2 National Educational Computing Conference, 1980</u>. University of Iowa: Iowa City, IA, 1980.

Papers delivered at second annual National Education Computing Conference.

762. Hasselbring, T., and J. Gray. "Using The Microcomputer for Assisting Teacher Decision Making." <u>Peabody Journal of Education</u> 62 (1984): 87-102.

Ways computers can aid teachers by providing data base type information for classroom instruction.

763. Hathaway, W.E. "Evolution, Nature, Uses and Issues In the Creation of Local School District Information Systems." Paper presented at the annual meeting of the American Educational Research Association, New Orleans, April 1984.

764. Hawkins, J., and K. Sheingold. "The Beginning of a Story: Computers and the Organization of Learning in Classrooms." <u>Microcomputers and Education. The Eighty Fifth Yearbook of the National Society for the Study of Education</u>. Edited by J. Culbertson and L. Cunningham. Chicago: University of Chicago Press, 1986.

765. Hayes, J. "Microcomputer Use In The Classroom, 1981-82." Paper presented at the annual convention of the National Audio Visual Association, Anaheim, CA, January 1982.

766. ______. "School Districts Using Microcomputers: A National Survey." Spectrum 1 (1983): 33-37.

Examines who, where, and how computer technology is used in schools.

767. Hazen, M. "An Argument in Favor of Multimethod Research and Evaluation in CAI and CMI Instruction." AEDS Journal 13 (1980): 275-284.

Discusses use of a variety of evaluative techniques in determining effectiveness of computer-assisted and computer-managed instruction.

768. HBJ Enterprises. "Computers in Public Education Study." ERIC ED 179 193, 1979.

769. Heinze-Fry, J. "Integration of Ausubelian Learning Theory and Educational Computing." American Biology Teacher 46 (1984): 152-156.

Analyzes use of advanced organizers as part of computer instructional applications.

770. Herman, J. Microcomputers in Schools: Toward More Effective Practices. California State University, Los Angeles. Center for the Study of Evaluation: Los Angeles, 1984.

Ways computers can be used in a more effective manner in schools.

771. Hickok, T.A. "Computer Education for Deaf Youngsters: A Mutual Effort by the University of California and The California School for the Deaf in Berkeley." Paper presented at the Association for the Development Of Computer Based Instructional Systems Summer Meeting, Portland, August 1975.

772. Hodes, C.L. "Relative Effectiveness of Corrective and Noncorrective Feedback in Computer Assisted Instruction on Learning and Achievement. Journal of Educational Technology Systems 13 (1985): 249-254.

Analyzes feedback learning theory and its applications to computer programs.

773. Hoffman, C. "Access and Equity: Computers for Everyone." Technological Horizons in Education 12 (1985): 72-74.

Who has computers and how they are using them in public schools.

774. Hoffman, J.L., and K. Waters. "Some Effects of Student Personality on Success with Computer Assisted Instruction." Educational Technology 17 (1982): 20-21.

What type of student uses computers both in classrooms and as part of their everyday experiences.

775. Hofmeister, A.M. Technological Tools for Rural Education. New Mexico Center For Rural Education: Las Cruces, NM, 1984.

Ways computers are being used to assist rural schools with limited budgets.

776. ______, and R. Throrkildsen. "Microcomputers In Special Education: Implications for Instructional Design." Exceptional Education Quarterly 4 (1984): 1-8.

Problems associated with designing instruction for special education students using technology.

777. Hooper, R. "To CAI Or Not To CAI?--That Is the Question." International Journal of Mathematical Education in Science and Technology 7 (1976): 461-473.

Discusses effectiveness of CAI in mathematical instruction.

778. Horack, V.M. "A Meta-Analysis of Research Findings on Individualized Instruction in Mathematics." Journal of Educational Research 74 (1981): 249-253.

As part of meta-analysis of individual instructional techniques, the effectiveness of CAI math programs is included. Findings indicate that most CAI school math programs are limited to development of basic skills.

779. Horn, C.E. "Light Mediated Learning Within the Computer Assisted Learning Environment." Pipeline 7 (1982): 7-9.

780. Howe, J. "Computer: A Researcher's View." Special Education: Forward Trends 7 (1980): 93-94.

Discusses research directions for computers and special education.

781. Hubert, H.A. "Computers and Composition: An Annotated Bibliography." ERIC ED 261 405, 1985.

782. Hudson, H.E., and C.H. Boyd. Distance Learning: A Review for Educators. Austin: Southwest Educational Development Laboratory, 1984.

Ways computers can be used as part of instruction in rural school settings.

783. Hunnes, F. "The Kelloggsville Story: Learning Management As a Means to More Effective Teaching of Reading." Phi Delta Kappan 60 (1978): 283-286.

Use of computers in teaching reading.

784. Hunter, B. Assessing the Impact, Benefits, Limitations and Costs of Computer Innovations In Education: A Retrospective Case Study Approach. Alexandria, VA: Human Resources Research Organization, 1979.

Case study of computer applications after they have been in use over a period of time.

785. Hurley, P., and D. Hlynka. "Prisoners of the Cave: Can Instructional Technology Improve Education." Paper presented at the National Conference on Instructional Technology, National Research Council of Canada, Manitoba, 1982.

786. Iakai, A. "Use of Computers in Education in Japan." ERIC ED 260 704, 1984.

787. Igntz, M.E. "Word Problem Solving with the APPLE II." Paper presented at the Florida Instructional Computing Conference, Orlando, FL, January 1982.

788. Ingersoll, G.M. "Microcomputers in American Public Schools: A National Survey." Educational Computer 3 (1983): 30-31.

Update on usage of microcomputers in public schools.

789. Ingle, H.T. Children' Perceptions of the Computer As an Expert Source of Information. Stanford University Center For Research and Development in Teaching: Palo Alto, CA, 1975.

How the computer affects children's perceptions of information dispensing and expertise.

790. Jelden, D.L. The Microcomputer As an Interactive Instructional System in the Classroom. Greeley, CO: University of Northern Colorado, 1980.

Ways in which microcomputers can be used as part of interactive instructional strategies.

791. Jensen, C.B. "Using What We've Learned in the Past To Improve the Future of Courseware Design." AEDS Journal 19 (1985): 28-48.

Analysis of computer courseware. Good points, bad points, and evaluation schema mentioned.

792. Jernstedt, G.C. "Active Learning Increases Educational Effectiveness and Efficiency." Technological Horizons in Education 9 (1982): 97-100, 105.

Use of technology as an active rather than a passive instructional tool.

793. Johansen, K.J., and R.D. Tennyson. "Effect of Adaptive Advisement on Perception in Learner Controlled, Computer Based Instruction Using a Rule-Learning Task. Educational Communication and Technology Journal 31 (1983): 226-236.

794. Kane, J.H. "Computers for Composing." Chameleon in The Classroom: Developing Roles for Computers. Edited by R. Case. New York: Bank Street College of Education, 1985.

Ways computers are used in the teaching of writing skills.

795. _____. "Microcomputer Technology in Schools: Issues for Research." Paper presented at the annual meeting of the American Educational Research Association, Montreal, April 1983.

796. Kansky, B. Instructional Computing in Wyoming: Status and Recommendations. University of Wyoming, Laramie, WY, 1981.

Current status report on computer and information system technological applications in Wyoming schools.

797. Kapp, A.B., and A.H. Knickerbocker. Computer Literacy and Development. A Project Report. Northeast Louisiana State University, Monroe, LA, 1983.

Development of methodologies to teach computer literacy.

798. Kearsley, G., B. Hunter, and R.J. Seidel. "Two Decades of Computer Based Instruction: What Have We Learned?" Technological Horizons in Education 10 (1983): 88-96.

Research overview of ten years of computer based instruction. Extensive bibliography and analysis of past studies provided.

799. Keegan, J.J., Jr. "The Role of High Technology in Salem Public School Classrooms." Spectrum 1 (1983): 33-36.

Applications of computer technology in classroom settings.

800. King, F.J., and M.D. Roblyer. "Alternative Designs for Evaluating Computer Based Instruction." Journal of Instructional Development 7 (1984): 23-29.

Differential evaluation designs for examining effectiveness of computer-based instruction.

801. Klaff, V., and P. Handler. "Computer Assisted Instruction of Population Dynamics: A New Approach to Population Education." ERIC ED 113 269, 1975.

802. Klein, R.D., and M. Thompson. "The Use of an Individualized Motivation System To Modify Accuracy and Rate on a Computer Based Number Facts Program." Paper presented at the annual meeting of the American Educational Research Association, San Francisco, April 1976.

803. King, R. "Information Systems and Policy Making: Computer Technology and Organizational Arrangements." Telecommunications Policy 2 (1978): 22-32.

Ways introduction of computers affect organizational and informational networks.

804. Knight, C.W., and G.E. Dunkelberger. "The Influence of Computer Managed Self-Paced Journalism on Science Attitudes Of Students." Journal of Research in Science Teaching 14 (1977): 551-555.

Analyzes effects on attitudes of students using computers. Positive and negative aspects of this type of learning environment.

805. Kolich, E. "Microcomputer Technology with the Learning Disabled: A Review of the Literature." Journal of Learning Disabilities 10 (1983): 79-86.

Review of research of computer applications for LD children.

806. Kollerbaur, A. "Computers in Swedish Schools: Experience, Research and Problems." Technological Horizons in Education 10 (1983): 79-86.

Description of computer utilization in Swedish schools.

807. Komoski, P. "Educational Computing: The Burden of Insuring Quality." Phi Delta Kappan 66 (1984): 244-248.

Ways to keep quality of instruction while using technology in classrooms.

808. Krueger, B. "Computerized Reporting in a Public School Program." Language, Speech and Hearing Services in the Schools 16 (1985): 135-139.

Use of computers as part of an information generating system.

809. Kulik, C., J. Kulik, and P. Cohen. "Instructional Technology and College Teaching." _Teaching of Psychology_ 7 (1980): 199-205.

How computers can be used in the teaching of psychology.

810. Kulik, J. "Integrating Findings from Different Levels of Instruction." Paper presented at the annual meeting of the American Educational Research Association, Los Angeles, April 1981.

811. ______. "Synthesis of Research on Computer Based Instruction." _Educational Leadership_ 41 (1983): 19-21.

Compendium of research reports on computers in schools and their effectiveness as an instructional tool.

812. Kurland, D.M., R. Mawbry, and N. Chair. "The Development of Programming Expertise in Adults and Children." Paper presented at the annual meeting of the American Educational Research Association, New Orleans, April 1984.

813. Lambright, W.H. _Educational Innovation As a Process of Coalition Building. A Study of Organizational Decision Making_. Syracuse Research Corporation: Syracuse, 1980.

How innovation affects decision making and its process.

814. Lansing, M.L. "Computers in Composition: A Bibliography of Research and Practice." ERIC ED 249 499, 1984.

815. Larson, H.J. _Analysis of Alternative Management Information Systems Appropriate for Special Education Application_. Walnut Creek, CA: Decision Development Corporation, 1981.

Description of CMI system used in special education environments.

816. Laudon, K. _Communications Technology and Democratic Participation_. New York: Praeger, 1977.

Discussion of the ways technology will affect governmental and political structures.

817. Lawler, R.W. "Extending A Powerful Idea. Artificial Intelligence Memo No. 590." ERIC ED 207 804, 1980.

818. Lawrence, B.F., and D.W. Spuck. "Numerical Procedures for Grouping Students for Instruction." AEDS Journal 12 (1979): 171-181.

819. Lawton, J., and V.T. Gerschner. "A Review of the Literature on Attitudes Towards Computers and Computerized Instruction." Journal of Research and Development in Education 16 (1982): 50-55.

820. Leeper, M. "Microcomputers in Education: Motivational and Social Issues." Paper presented at the annual meeting of the American Psychological Association, Washington, DC, August 1982.

821. ______. "Microcomputers in Education." Paper presented at the annual meeting of the American Educational Research Association, Washington, DC, April 1983.

822. ______. "Microcomputers in Education: Motivational and Social Issues." American Psychologist 40 (1985): 1-18.

How microcomputers affect student motivation towards learning and school in general.

823. Leiblum, M.D. "Computer Managed Instruction: An Explanation and Overview." AEDS Journal 15 (1982): 126-142.

Ways that CMI affects classrooms in terms of instructional organization.

824. ______. "A Media Selection Model Geared Toward CAL." Technological Horizons in Education 7 (1980): 29-33.

Ideas used in selecting courseware for computer-assisted learning.

825. Lesgold, A.M., and F. Reif. Computers in Education: Realizing the Potential. Philadelphia: American Society of Educators, 1983.

Directions schools might take in using computers.

826. Levim, J.A., and Y. Kareev. Personal Computers and Education: The Challenge to Schools. La Jolla, CA: University of California, San Diego, Center for Human Information Processing, 1980.

How schools can effectively utilize computers over the next decade.

827. Levin, D. "In This System, The Computer Future Is Now." American School Board Journal 169 (1982): 27-28.

Analysis of a school district currently implementing computer technology in its classroom.

828. Levin, H.M. Towards a Meta-Cost-Effectiveness Analysis of Educational Interventions. Palo Alto, CA: The Institute for Research on Educational Finance and Governance, School of Education, Stanford University, 1981.

Analyzes cost effectiveness of technological interventions.

829. ______. Cost and Cost Effectiveness of Computer Assisted Instruction. Palo Alto, CA: The Institute for Research on Educational Finance and Governance, School of Education, Stanford University, 1984.

Analysis of true costs of computers in schools including training, hardware, and psychic costs.

830. ______. "Cost Effectiveness of Four Educational Interventions." ERIC ED 246 533, 1984.

831. ______, and G. Meister. "Is CAI Cost-Effective?" Phi Delta Kappan 67 (1986): 745-749.

832. ______, and R. Rumberger. The Educational Implications of High Technology. Palo Alto, CA: The Institute for Research on Educational Finance and Governance, School of Education, Stanford University, 1983.

833. ______, and L. Woo. An Evaluation of the Costs of Computer Assisted Instruction. Palo Alto, CA: The Institute for Research on Educational Finance and Governance, School of Education, Stanford University, 1980.

834. Lewis, R. "Teachers, Pupils and Microcomputers." Technological Horizons in Education 10 (1983): 81-87.

Effects of introduction of computers on these two groups.

835. Lidtke, D.K. "Securing Teacher Acceptance of Technology." Paper presented at the National Conference on Technology and Education, Washington, DC, January 1981.

836. Liebling, C.R. "Creating the Classroom's Communicative Context: How Parents, Teachers and Microcomputers Can Help." ERIC ED 240 509, 1984.

837. Lilie, D.L. "Comparison Of Microcomputer Generated IEPs and Teacher Written IEPs: A Pilot Study." Paper presented at the annual convention of the Association for Children and Adults with Learning Disabilities, Washington, DC, February 1983.

838. Linn, M.C. "Fostering Equitable Consequences from Computer Learning Environments." Paper presented at the annual midyear conference of the American Educational Research Association Research on Women and Education Special Interest Group, Tempe, AZ, November 1983.

839. ______. "The Cognitive Consequences of Programming Instructions in Classrooms." Educational Researcher 14 (1985): 14-16, 25-29.

Different types of computer programs and the ways they affect thinking and skill development.

840. Lipkin, J. Equity and Microcomputer Use in American Public Education. Denver, CO: Education Commission of the States, 1983.

Discussion of schools and individuals who have access to computers and those who do not. Mentions implications for educational and social policy.

841. ______. "Equity in Computer Education." Educational Leadership 41 (1983): 26.

Who has computers and how they are using them in schools.

842. Lipson, J.I. Educational Technology in Vocational Education. Columbus, OH: National Center for Research in Vocational Education, 1984.

Ways computers are being used in vocational training programs nationwide.

843. Lockheed, M.E. Determinants of Student Computer Use: An Analysis of Data from the 1984 National Assessment of Educational Progress. Princeton, NJ: Educational Testing Service, 1985.

Presents ways that students use computers both in and out of school.

844. ______. "Women, Girls and Comptuers: A First Look at the Evidence." Sex Roles 13 (1985): 115-122.

Discusses how women and girls are using computers, their ability to access them, and educational implications.

845. ______, and S.B. Frakt. "Sex Equity: Increasing Girls' Use of Computers." The Computing Teacher 8 (1984): 23-26.

See item #844.

846. ______, A. Neilson, and M.K. Stone. "Sex Differences in Microcomputing Literacy." Proceedings of NECC/5 National Educational Computing Conference, 1983. Edited by D. Bonnette. Silver Springs, MD: IEEE Computer Society Press, 1983.

Paper/symposium presented at the fifth annual National Education Computing Conference.

847. Loftus, W.J. "A User's Balance Sheet on Computer Assisted Learning." Technological Horizons in Education 10 (1982): 118-123.

Effectiveness of computer instruction from a student perspective.

848. Loop, L., and P. Christensen. Exploring the Microcomputer Learning Environment. San Francisco, CA: Far West Laboratory for Educational Research and Development, 1980.

Ways schools use microcomputers as part of the learning process.

849. Loughlin, T. "Educating Maladjusted Pupils With Microcomputers." Paper presented at the British Psychological Society, Division of Educational and Child Psychology, Annual Refresher Course, Southhampton, January 1984.

850. Lynch, W.W. "CATTS Technology in Analyzing Observational Data from Public School Classrooms: A Study Of Interactive Tactics and Decisions of Teachers." Paper presented at the annual meeting of the American Educational Research Association, New York, April 1977.

851. Macken, E. "Considerations in Evaluating Individualized Instruction." _Journal of Research and Development in Education_ 14 (1980): 79-83.

Ways to evaluate individual learning environments including computer augmented ones.

852. Magidson, E.M. "Trends in Computer Assisted Instruction." _Educational Technology_ 18 (1978): 45-48.

853. Malone, T.W. _What Makes Things Fun To Learn? A Study of Intrinsically Motivating Computer Games_. Palo Alto, CA: Xerox Palo Alto Research Center, 1980.

Presents criteria for successful video and computer game development.

854. _____, P. Suppes, M. Zanott, and L. Kanevera. "Projecting Student Trajectories in a Computer Assisted Instruction Curriculum." _Journal of Educational Psychology_ 71 (1979): 74-84.

Analyzes student decision-making paradigms in CAI instruction.

855. Mandinach, E.B. "Clarifying The "A" in CAI for Learners of Different Abilities." Paper presented at the annual meeting of the American Educational Research Association, New Orleans, April 1984.

856. _____. "Cognitive Consequences Of Microcomputer Applications." Paper presented at the Computers and Com-

plex Thinking Conference, Washington, DC, October, 1985.

857. ______, and L. Corno. Ability and Gender As Influences On Student Engagement In Computer Solving Instruction. Palo Alto, CA: Stanford University, School of Education, 1984.

Analyzes gender differences in problem-solving situations using interactive technology.

858. ______, and C.W. Fisher. Review of Research on the Cognitive Effects of Computer Assisted Learning. Berkeley, CA: University of California, 1983.

Overview of research in cognition and computer-assisted learning.

859. Market Data Retrieval. Update on the School Masrket for Microcomputers. Westport, CT: Market Retrieval Data, Inc., 1982.

Profiles of purchasers and types of microcomputers they are buying.

860. Mason, G.E. Computer Applications In Reading. Newark, DE: International Reading Association, 1983.

Update on how computers are being used in reading instruction.

861. Mawby, R. "Determining Students' Understanding of Programming Concepts." Paper presented at the annual meeting of the American Educational Research Association, New Orleans, April 1984.

862. McCann, P.H. "Learning Strategies and Computer Based Education." Computers and Education 5 (1981): 133-140.

Ways students use computers as part of their learning skills.

863. McCaslin, P., and L. Stevens. "Immediate Openings." Pointer 28 (1984): 16-19.

Notes need for teachers for computer-based classrooms.

864. McConnell, B.B. "Evaluation of Computer Assisted Instruction in Math, Pasco School District Final Report." ERIC ED 235 959, 1983.

865. McCullough, C.S., and L.S. Wenck. "Current Microcomputer Applications in School Psychology." <u>School Psychology Review</u> 13 (1984): 429-439.

Ways computers are being used by school psychologists including testing and data storage.

866. McLaughlin, P. "Computer-Based Education. The Best of ERIC, 1983-1985." ED 284542, 1986.

867. McPhail, I. "Computer Inequities in School Uses of Microcomputers: Policy Implications." <u>Journal of Negro History</u> 54 (1985): 3-13.

Discussion of minorities and computer accession in school situations.

868. Megarry, J. <u>Computers and Education. World Yearbook of Education 1982/83</u>. New York: Nichols Publishing Co., 1983.

Ways computers are being used throughout the world in a variety of educational settings.

869. Menis, Y., M. Snyder, and E. Ben-Kohav. "Improving Achievement by Means of the Computer." <u>Educational Technology</u> 20 (1980): 32-36.

How computers can raise achievement scores.

870. Merrill, M.D. "Learner Control and Computer Based Learning." <u>Instructional Development: The State of the Art II</u>. Edited by B.K. Bass and C.R. Dills. Dubuque, IA: Kendall/Hunt Publishing Co., 1984.

Effects of learners controlling their environment and the cognitive consequences of this situation.

871. Merrill, P.F., and D. Salisbury. "Research on Drill and Practice Strategies." <u>Journal of Computer Based Instruction</u> 11 (1984): 19-21.

Provides analysis of the usefulness of drill and practice in certain learning situations.

872. Mevarech, Z.R. "Computer Assisted Instructional Methods: A Factorial Study Within Mathematics Disadvantaged Classrooms." Journal of Experimental Education 54 (1985): 22-27.

873. Meyer, R.S., and P.A. Caldwell. "Transformation." Computers and Education 7 (1983): 69-78.

How computers are changing school learning environments.

874. Micro-Ideas. "Proceedings of The Annual Conference on The Role of the Computer in Education." ERIC ED 260 702, 1985.

875. Miller, I. Microcomputers and The Media Specialist: Annotated Bibliography. Syracuse, NY: Information Resources Publications, 1981.

Use of computers by media specialists as described in articles, books, and reviews.

876. Milner, J.D. "Micro to Main Frame Computers in English Education." North Carolina English Teacher 39 (1982): 1-45.

Ways computers can be used in the English classroom.

877. Miura, I. Home Computer Ownership: Does It Effect Computer Interest and Usage? Palo Alto, CA: Stanford University, School Of Education, 1984.

878. ______, R.D. Hess. "Sex Differences in Computer Access, Interst and Usage." Paper presented at the annual meeting of the American Psychological Association, Anaheim, CA, August 1983.

879. Moe, D.J. "The Effects Of Sex, Residence Status, Grade Level and Usage Level on Computer Equity." ERIC ED 255 182, 1984.

880. Molnar, A.R. "The Search for New Intellectual Technologies." Technological Horizons in Education 10 (1982): 104-112.

Use of artificial intelligence in computer programming.

881. Montgomeris, T.C. Telidon Distance Education Field Trial. Alberta Department of Education: Edmonton, Alberta, 1982.

Computers used in rural settings as part of a distance education program.

882. Moore, J. "Computer Series 5: Computer Aided Instruction with Microcomputers. Part I Systems and Applications." Journal of Chemical Education 56 (1979): 776-783.

Use of computers in the teaching of chemistry.

883. Morgan, C.E. "Effectiveness Of Technology in the Schools--Public and Taxpayers Response." Paper presented at the National Conference on Technology and Education, Washington, DC, 1981.

884. ____. Evaluation of Computer Assisted Instruction, 1975-76. Rockville, MD: Montgomery County Public Schools, 1977.

Use of computers in a school district over the course of a single year.

885. Moshell, M. "The Intelligence Amplifier: An Essay On The Design Of Computer Based Curricula." The Computing Teacher 10 (1982): 57-61.

Description of instructional design techniques used in writing computer software.

886. Moskowitz, J., and B. Birman. "Computers in the Schools: Implications for Change." Educational Technology 25 (1985): 7-14.

Ways computers can affect overall school environments.

887. Mosley, M.L. "Computer Assisted Instruction and Continuing Motivation." Paper presented at the annual meeting

of the Association for Educational Communications and Technology, Dallas, January 1984.

888. Mravetz, P.J. "The Effects of Computer Assisted Instruction on Student Self Concept, Locus of Control, Level of Aspiration, and Reading Achievement." Ph.D. dissertation. University of Akron, 1980.

889. Mulligan, J.G. "A Cost Function for Computer Assisted Programmed Instruction." Journal of Economic Education 15 (1984): 275-281.

890. Napier, J.D. "Computer Literacy and Social Studies Education: Changes in Form and Content." Paper presented at Consortium, Athens, GA, June 1983.

How not being computer literate affects the social studies classroom now and in the future.

891. National Association of State Directors of Special Education. First Special Education Technology Research and Development Symposium. Washington, DC: National Association of State Directors of Special Education, 1984.

Papers describing research into uses of computers in special education settings.

892. National Center for Education Statistics. Instructional Use of Computers in Public Schools. Washington, DC: Office for Educational Statistics, 1982.

How schools are using computers in a variety of content areas.

893. National Education Association. A Teacher Survey NEA Report: Computers in the Classroom. Washington, DC: National Education Association, 1983.

894. National Educational Computing Conference. "Conference Abstracts: NECC '82." Journal of Computers in Mathematics and Science Teaching 2 (1982).

895. National School Boards Association. School/Home Computer Survey. Alexandria, VA: National School Boards Association, 1984.

Ways that computers are being used in schools and in children's homes.

896. Nelson, P., and W. Waack. "The Status of Computer Literacy/Computer Assisted Instruction Awareness As a Factor in Classroom Instruction and Teacher Selection." Educational Technology 25 (1985): 23-26.

Discusses research on how computer literate teachers function over those not trained in technology. Implications for hiring of future teachers.

897. Neuman, D. "Learning Disabilities and Microcomputer Courseware: A Qualitative Study Of Students' and Teachers' Interactions with Instructional Dimensions." Paper presented at the annual meeting of the American Educational Research Association, Chicago, April 1985.

898. New York State Education Department. Report on the Statewide Instructional Computing Network's 1st Annual Survey of Instructional Computing Practices/Plans of New York State School Districts. Albany, NY: New York State Education Department, 1982.

899. Ngaiyaye, M.S.W., and A. VanderPloge. "Differential Effectiveness of Three Kinds of Computer-Assisted Instruction." Paper presented at the annual meeting of the American Educational Research Association, San Francisco, 1986.

900. Nolan, F. "CAI in Mathematical Problem Solving: Guidelines for Software Design and Purchase." Computers in The Schools 1 (1984): 71-80.

What to look for in good software for problem-solving situations.

901. Noonan, J.V. "Feedback Procedures in Computer Assisted Instruction: Knowledge-of-Results, Knowledge-of-Correct-Response, Process Explanations, and Second Attempts After Errors." Ph.D. dissertation. University of Illinois at Urbana-Champaign, 1984.

902. Norris, C.M., and B. Lumsden. "Functional Distance and the Attitudes of Educators Toward Computers." Technological Horizons in Education 11 (1984): 129-132.

Analyzes attitudes of educators towards computer use.

903. Norris, W. "Improving Education Through Technological Innovation." Technological Horizons in Education 12 (1985): 65-68.

Ways technology can affect schools positively.

904. Office of Technology Assessment. Information Technology and Its Impact On American Education. Washington, DC: Congressional Office of Technological Assessment, 1982.

Ways that all types of information technology are being used in schools. Includes case studies of schools using computers in a variety of formats.

905. Ohlsson, S. "Computer Simulation and Its Impact on Educational Research and Practice." ED 282521, 1985.

906. Ojeda, E. "Effectiveness of a Computer Assisted Instruction Supported Bilingual Program for Hispanic Students." Ph.D. dissertation. Wayne State University, 1984.

907. Ogletree, E.J., and T.C. Haskins. "A Survey of Microcomputer Use in Illinois School Districts." ERIC ED 252 189, 1983.

908. ______, and T.C. Haskins. "Microcomputer Use in Schools: A Research Review." ERIC ED 252 187, 1983.

909. Olson, D. "Computer As a tool of the Intellect." Educational Researcher 14 (1985): 5-70.

Essay on the use of computers and technology as part of the problem-solving process.

910. Olson, J.L. "CATTS (Computer Assisted Teacher Training System) Technical Configuration and Application to Research on Reading." Paper presented at the annual meeting of the American Educational Research Association, NY, April 1977.

911. O'Neal, F. "An Alternative Model for Computer Assisted Instruction in an Educational Environment." *Technological Horizons in Education* 11 (1984): 113-117.

Group computer work stations as an alternative to individualized modes.

912. O'Neil, H.F. *Computer Based Instruction: A State of the Art Assessment*. New York: Academic Press, 1981.

Current status of instructional uses of computers in schools.

913. ______, and J. Paris. "Introduction and Overview of Computer Based Instruction." *Computer Based Instruction: A State of the Art Assessment*. Edited by H.F. O'Neil. New York: Academic Press, 1981.

History of computer-based instruction including its psychological background.

914. Orlansky, J. "Effectiveness of CAI: A Different Finding." *Electronic Learning* 3 (1983): 58, 60.

Some CAI modes are not helpful in increasing instructional understanding.

915. Orlov, I.A. "A Computer Investigation on the Educational Process." *Soviet Education* 18 (1976): 67-82.

Uses of computers in Soviet schools.

916. O'Shea, T. *Self-Improving Teaching Systems: An Application of Artificial Intelligence To Computer Assisted Instruction*. Boston: Birkhauser Books, 1979.

917. ______, and J. Self. *Learning and Teaching with Computers*. Englewood Cliffs, NJ: Prentice-Hall, 1983.

918. Papert, S. "New Theories for New Learning." *School Psychology Review* 13 (1984): 422-428.

Application of individual learning theory and CAI.

919. Parry, J.D., and J.M. Ferrara. *The Potential of Computer Based Expert Systems for Special Educators in Rural Settings*. Logan, UT: Utah State University, 1984.

920. Patterson, J.H., and M.S. Smith. "The Role of Computers in Higher Order Thinking Processes." Paper presented at the Computers and Complex Thinking Conference, Washington, DC, October 1985.

921. Pea, R.D. Prospects and Challenges For Using Microcomputers in School. New York: Bank Street College of Education, Center for Children and Technology, 1984.

922. ______, and D.M. Kurland. "On the Cognitive Effects of Learning Computer Programming." New Ideas in Psychology 2 (1984): 137-168.

How learning computer programming affects the cognitive processes especially the problem-solving processes.

923. Pederson, J.K., and D.J. DeGuire. "VCR Microcomputer Teaching/Inservice." Paper presented at the annual Rural and Small Schools Conference, Manhattan, KS, November 1982.

924. Pennington, N. Cognitive Components of Expertise in Computer Programming. A Review of the Literature. Ann Arbor, MI: University of Michigan Center for Cognitive Science, 1982.

925. Perez, E.C., and M.A. White. "Student Evaluation of Motivation and Learning Attributes of Microcomputer Software." Journal of Computer Based Instruction 12 (1985): 39-43.

How students rate different types of computer software.

926. Perkins, D.N. "The Fingertip Effect: How Information Processing Shapes Thinking." Educational Researcher 14 (1985): 11-17.

Discussion of information processing and cognition through the use of technology.

927. Pitts, M.R. A Bright Promise but a Dim Future. Researchers Examine the Potential of Educational Technology. Washington, DC: Council For Educational Development and Research, 1981.

Review of current usage of computers in schools and implications for their future applications.

928. Plienis, A.J., and R.G. Romanczyk. Teacher Versus Computer Delivered Instruction: An Analysis of Child Performance Behavior and Characteristics. Albany: State of New York, Albany Research Foundation, 1982.

929. Ponchilla, S.K. "A Comparison of Computer Assisted Instruction and Traditional Instruction in Braille Transcription." Ph.D. dissertation. Western Michigan University, 1984.

930. Pool, I. de S. "What Ferment? A Challenge for Empirical Research." Journal of Communication 33 (1983): 258-261.

Discusses effectiveness of computers in schools and research directions.

931. Pressman, I., and B. Rosenbloom. "CAI: Its Role and Its Cost." Journal of Educational Technology Systems 12 (1984): 183-208.

Analyzes role for CAI and its overall cost effectiveness.

932. Quality Education Data, Inc. Microcomputer Usage in Schools, 1983-84. Denver, CO: Quality Education Data, Inc., 1984.

Survey of ways microcomputers are being used in school settings.

933. ______. Microcomputer Usage in Schools, 1984-85. Denver, CO: Quality Education Data, Inc., 1985.

Update of item #932.

934. Quinsatt, M.Q. "Implementing Computer Technology In Classroom Settings: An Anecdotal Report of Long Term Use." Paper presented at the National Institute for Education Conference on Implementing Computer Technology in Classroom Settings, Washington, DC, 1981.

935. Ragosta, M. "Computer Assisted Instruction and Compensatory Education: A Longitudinal Analysis." Machine-Mediated Learning 1 (1983): 97-127.

Analysis of computer usage in compensatory math and reading programs.

936. Rapaport, P., and W.G. Savard. Computer Assisted Instruction. Research On School Effectiveness Project: Topic Summary Report. Portland, OR: Northwest Educational Regional Laboratory, 1980.

Use of CAI as part of increasing school performance and learning.

937. Reeves, T.C., and R.M. Lent. "Levels of Evaluation for Computer Based Instruction." Instructional Software: Principles and Perspectives for Design and Use. Edited by D.F. Walker and R.D. Hess. Belmont, CA: Wadsworth Publishing Co., 1984.

Discussion of evaluation techniques and design options for computer courseware.

938. Reid, J.P. Identification of Computer Software for the Disadvantaged and Compatible Hardware. Indiana, PA: Indiana University of Pennsylvania, 1983.

939. Reil, M., and M. Cole. Mislabeled But Not Misidentified. San Diego, Laboratory of Comparative Human Cognition, 1982.

Ways computers can be used to identify learning styles and problem learners.

940. Reinking. D. "On Conceptualizing Research Methodologies For Computer Based Instruction." Paper presented at the International Conference for Development Of Computer Based Instructional Systems, Philadelphia, March 1985.

941. Revelle, G., M. Honey, E. Amsel, L. Schauble, and G. Levine. "Sex Differences in the Use of Computers." Paper presented at the annual meeting of the American Educational Research Association, New Orleans, April 1984.

942. Riley, D.C. "Computer Assisted Evaluation at the California School for the Deaf-Fremont." American Annals of the Deaf 128 (1983): 585-594.

Computers used in deaf education instructional format.

943. Roblyer, M.D. Measuring the Impact of Computers in Education: A Non-Technical Review of Research for Educators. Washington, DC: Association for Educational Data Systems, 1985.

Effectiveness of computer technology as reported in research studies extending over the past five years.

944. Rogers, E.M., J. McManus, J.D. Peters, and J.I. Kim. Microcomputers in the Schools: A Case Of Decentralized Diffusion. Palo Alto: Stanford University, Institution For Communication Research, 1984.

Case study of effects of microcomputers as an educational innovation.

945. Rose, S., and M. Waldron. "Microcomputer Use in Programs for Hearing Impaired Children: A National Survey." American Annals of the Deaf 129 (1984): 338-342.

Uses of information technology for deaf and hearing-impaired children as reported from a national survey.

946. Rosenberg, M.S., and P.T. Sindelar. "Computer Assisted Data Management of Instructional Programming." Education Unlimited 86 (1981): 37-40.

Description of data management system for use within instructional sequences. Computers used in managing and storing instructional data.

947. Rossmiller, R., and W. Otto. "Wisconsin Research and Development Center for Individualized Schooling. Bibliography of Publications." ERIC ED 163 944, 1978.

948. Rothenberg, D., and R.P. Morgan. Case Studies of Innovation in the Educational Service Sector. St. Louis: Washington University Center for Development Technology, 1975.

Use of computers and technology in schools as part of an overall research study on the effects of school innovations.

949. Rubin, S.E. "Public Schools Should Learn to Ski...and Other Helpful Hints for Educating in the 21st Century." Paper presented at the National Curriculum Study Institute, Phoenix, January 1981.

950. Ryan, S.K. "CAM Challenges Students To Perform Better." Educational Leadership 57 (1980): 590-593.

Ways CMI affects student performance and achievement.

951. Sadowski, B.R., and C. Lovett. Using Computers To Enhance Teaching and Improve Teacher Centers. Houston: University of Houston, 1981.

Use of computers as part of teacher center inservice training programs.

952. Sakamoto, T. "Evaluation Methods for Improving CAL Materials." Computers and Education 3 (1979): 281-291.

Discussion of evaluation techniques available for use in reviewing computer-assisted learning materials.

953. Sales, G.C., C.A. Carrier, and A.D. Glenn. "Evaluating Lessons That Use Computers." The Computing Teacher 13 (1986): 84-90.

954. Salisbury, D.F. "Using Microcomputers for Drill and Practice: Issues and Implications." Paper presented at the Annual Convention of the Association for Educational Communications and Technology, Anaheim, CA, January 1985.

955. Salomon, G. Interaction of Media, Cognition and Learning. San Francisco, CA: Jossey-Bass, 1979.

Ways in which media affect learning styles. Discussion of microcomputers and computers included.

956. ______. "Television Is "Easy" and Print Is "Tough": The Differential Investment of Mental Effort in Learning As a Function of Perceptions and Attributions." Journal of Educational Psychology 76 (1984): 647-658.

Difference in learning styles as related to use of media. Notes implications for computer uses.

957. ______, and R.E. Clark. "Reexamining The Methodology of Research On Media and Technology in Education." _Review of Educational Research_ 47 (1977): 99-120.

Studies of the effectiveness of media in classroom situations. Notes implications for computers.

958. ______, and H. Gardner. _The Computer As Educator: Lessons from Television Research_. Cambridge: Harvard University, Graduate School of Education, 1984.

Discussion of research on the effectiveness of television as an educational aid as related to use of the computer in similar configurations.

959. Sardello, R.J. "The Technological Threat to Education." _Teachers College Record_ 85 (1984): 631-639.

Analysis of how technology may affect schooling in a humanistic format.

960. Savard, W.G., and K. Cotton. "What Effective Schooling Research Says to Migrant Education Program Planners." Paper presented at the annual Migrant Education Conference, Portland, OR, May 1983.

961. Schiffman, G. "Microcomputer Instruction for the Learning Disabled." _Journal of Learning Disabilities_ 15 (1982): 557-559.

Ways microcomputers can be used with learning disabled students.

962. ______. "Personal Computers for the Learning Disabled." _Journal of Learning Disabilities_ 15 (1982): 422-425.

Description of computer programs for children with learning disabilities.

963. Schimizzi, N.V. _Microcomputers in the Schools_. Buffalo: State University of New York at Buffalo, 1983.

Survey of uses of microcomptuers in public schools.

964. Schimmel, B.J. "A Meta Analysis of Feedback to Learners in Computerized and Programmed Instruction." Paper presented at the annual meeting of the American Educational Research Association, Montreal, April 1983.

965. Schloss, P.J. "Questions and Highlights In CAI Modules." <u>The Computing Teacher</u> 12 (1985): 14-15.

Use of questions and questioning techniques in CAI materials.

966. Schmidt, M. "Computer-Assisted Instruction with Exceptional Children." <u>Journal of Special Education</u> 19 (1986): 493-501.

Meta-analysis of studies on effectiveness of CAI with exceptional children show only a moderate effect for CAI versus traditionl instruction.

967. Schoen, H.L., and T.C. Hunt. "The Effect of Technology on Instruction: The Literature of the Last Twenty Years." <u>AEDS Journal</u> 10 (1977): 68-82.

Research review of information technology and its effects on the schooling processes over the past two decades.

968. Schubert, J.G. "Females and Microcomputers Use In School: Some Insights Into Traditional Patterns." Paper presented at the annual meeting of the American Educational Research Association, New Orleans, April 1984.

969. Schuelke, D., and D.T. King. "New Technology in the Classroom: Computers and Communication and The Future." <u>Technological Horizons in Education</u> 10 (1983): 95-100.

Looks at future applications of technology in educational settings.

970. Schulz, D.G. "Teachers Adapt To Innovation." ERIC ED 185 495, 1979.

971. Scurlock, B.L. "The Effects of Sibling Rank, Age, Sex, and Attitude on the Achievement Gain Of Basic Mathematics Students Taught by a Computer Assisted Instruction and Prescription Learning Program." Ph.D. dissertation. University of Miami, 1984.

972. Seidel, R.J., and L. Stolurow. "A Heuristic Meta Model for Computer Managed Instruction." Journal of Educational Research and Development 14 (1980): 16-32.

Ways to apply computer-managed applications. Models for CMI included.

973. Semmel, M.I. "The Improvement Of Social Studies Among Rejected Pupils Through the Modification of Teacher Behavior Using The Computer Assisted Teacher Training System (CATTS): An Inservice Training Application of CATTS." ERIC ED 162 469, 1976.

974. Semple, E. Jr. "Garfield Computer Survey-1983." ERIC ED 243 461, 1983.

975. Seymour, S.L. "Microcomputers and Continuing Motivation." Paper presented at the annual convention of the Association for Educational Communications and Technology, Las Vegas, 1986.

976. Shavelson, R.J. "Teachers' Instructional Uses of Microcomputers." Paper presented at the annual meeting of the American Educational Research Association, Montreal, April 1983.

977. ______, and G. Salomon. "Information Technology: Tool and Teacher of the Mind." Educational Researcher 14 (1985): 4-5.

Ties together computer technology and cognitive development.

978. Sheingold, K. Issues Related to the Implementation of Computer Technology in Schools: A Cross-Sectional Study. New York: Bank Street College of Education, 1981.

Difficulties in implementation of computer technology in educational environments.

979. ______. "Chameleon in the Classroom: Developing Roles for Computers." ERIC ED 249 921, 1983.

980. ______, J.H. Kane, and M.E. Endreweit. "Microcomputer Use in Schools: Developing a Research Agenda." Harvard Educational Review 53 (1983): 412-432.

Overview of research studies involving computer technology and possibilities for future research.

981. Simon, H.A. "The Computer Age." Computers In Education: Realizing the Potential. Washington, DC: United States Department of Education, 1983.

Ways to use computer technology in educational settings.

982. Sims, D. "A Pilot Experiment in Computer Assisted Speech Reading Instruction Utilizing the Data Analysis Interactive Device (DAVID)." American Annals of the Deaf 124 (1979): 618-623.

Discusses and analyzes voice synthesizers and computers as tools in deaf education.

983. Singer, B. "A Formative and Summative Evaluation of Computer Integrated Instruction." Paper presented at the Computer Based Education Conference, Washington, DC, January 1982.

984. Singer, H., and P. Phelps. "The History of Computers and Their Use in Education." Paper presented at the annual meeting of the National Reading Conference, Austin,, December 1982.

985. Smith, R.L. "Bibliography--Simulation, Part I." Journal of Computers in Mathematics and Science Teaching 1 (1982): 34-35.

Bibliography of computer simulations including evaluative notations.

986. Sommers, E.A., and J.L. Collins. "What Research Tells Us About Composing and Computing." ERIC ED 249 497, 1984.

987. Southwest Educational Development Laboratory. R & D Speaks: Effectiveness of Microcomputers in Educational Applications. Austin, TX: Southwest Educational Development Laboratory, 1983.

Overview of research in computer assisted instruction. Discusses effectiveness in several environments.

988. Spatz, V. "Computers and Equity." Equity and Choice 1 (1985): 52-54.

Discussion of equity issues in computer education in terms of who has computers and how they are being used.

989. Spencer, M., and L. Baskin. "Classroom Computers: Do They Make a Difference?" Classroom Computer News 2 (1981): 12-15, 8.

Rationale for using computers in classroom situations.

990. Spero, S.W. "Instructional Computing Systems in Israel: A Learning Experience and Teaching Experience." Journal of Educational Technology Systems 6 (1978): 33-44.

Computer and information technology uses in Israeli schools.

991. Springer, D.M. "School District Computer Use Survey/ Results." AEDS Monitor 20 (1982): 28-31.

Survey of computer uses including instructional and management queries.

992. Sproull, L.S., and K.R. Hofmeister. Implementation: A Cognitive Perspective. Pittsburgh, PA: Carnegie-Mellon University, 1982.

Cognitive effects of computer and technological introductions in school environments.

993. Spuck, D.W., and W.C. Bozeman. "Pilot Test and Evaluation of a System of Computer Managed Instruction." AEDS Journal 12 (1978): 31-41.

Analyzes effectiveness of CMI system.

994. ______, and W.C. Bozeman. "A Design for the Evaluation of Management Information Systems." AEDS Journal 14 (1980): 30-40.

Description of information evaluation systems for use in schools.

995. Stasz, C. "Teachers As Role Models: Are Three Gender Differences in Microcomputer Based Mathematics and Science Instruction?" Sex Roles 13 (1985): 149-164.

Analyzes gender differences in using and discussing computers and technology.

996. Steele, K.J. "The Effect of Computer Assisted Mathematical Instruction upon the Computer Literacy of Fifth Grade Students Using a Microcomputer." Ph.D. dissertation. University of Oregon, 1984.

997. Stegman, M.O. "Beyond Correctness: The Computer and the Composing Process." Paper presented at the Spring Writing Conference of the New York State Department of Education, Albany, May 1984.

998. Steinberg, E.R. "Review of Student Control in Computer Assisted Instruction." Journal of Computer Based Instruction 3 (1977): 84-90.

Locus of control in students using computers as part of their instructional interactions.

999. Stennett, R.G. Computer Assisted Instruction: A Review of the Reviews. London, Ontario: London Board of Education. Educational Research Services, 1985.

Discusses review of research literature on computer-assisted instruction.

1000. Stevens, D.J. "How Educators Perceive Computers in the Classroom." AEDS Journal 13 (1980): 221-232.

1001. _____, and W. Sybouts. "Computers In The Classroom." Clearing House 56 (1982): 82-85.

Uses of computers in a variety of classroom situations.

1002. Stimmel, T., J. Common, B. McCaskill, and H.J. Durrett. "Teacher Resistance To Computer Assisted Instruction." Behavior Research Methods and Instrumentation 13 (1981): 128-130.

Reasons teachers refuse to accept computers in their classrooms. Includes ties to implementation of innovations.

1003. Stodolsky, D. "Automatic Facilitation of Dialogue in Shy and Not Shy Problem Solving Teams." Paper presented at the annual meeting of the Western Psychological Association, San Diego, April 1979.

1004. Stone, D.C. "An Intelligent CAI System For Diagnostic Testing and Instruction." Ph.D. dissertation. University of Pennsylvania, 1985.

1005. Strehlo, K. "The Electronic Schoolhouse Graduates Better Thinkers." Personal Computing 7 (1983): 66-67, 71-72, 74, 196.

Cognitive skills and how they are related to computer usage.

1006. Stromberg, L., and R.J. Kurth. "Using Word Processing To Teach Revision in Written Composition." Paper presented at the annual meeting of the National Reading Conference, Austin, December 1983.

1007. Sturdivant, P. "Houston Researchers' Computer Supported Immersion Strategy." AEDS Monitor 21 (1983): 25-27.

Discussion of implementation of computers in a large public school system.

1008. Suppes, P. Current Trends in Computer Assisted Instruction. New York: Academic Press, 1979.

Overview of how computers are being used in schools and types of computer-assisted instructional processes being implemented.

1009. Swadener, M. Personal Computers and Cross-Aged Instruction, First Year Report. Boulder: University of Colorado, 1981.

Uses of computers in a variety of settings across age groups.

1010. Taber, F.M. "MCE Field Study Report." Paper presented at the national convention for the Council for Exceptional Children, Houston, February 1982.

1011. Tawney, J.W., and G.P. Cartwright. "Teaching in a Technology Oriented Society." <u>Teacher Education and Special Education</u> 4 (1981): 3-14.

How technology affects the special education classroom.

1012. Tennyson, R.D. "Advisement and Management Strategies As Design Variables in Computer Assisted Instruction." <u>Educational Communication and Technology: A Journal of Theory, Research and Development</u> 28 (1980): 169-176.

1013. ______. "Use of Adaptive Information for Advisement in Learning Concepts and Rules Using Computer Assisted Instruction." <u>American Educational Research Journal</u> 18 (1981): 425-438.

1014. ______, and R. Park. "Computer Based Adaptive Instructional Systems: A Review of Empirically Based Models." <u>Machine Mediated Learning</u> 1 (1984): 158-170.

Use of computers in a variety of instructional systems.

1015. ______, and R. Park. "Process Learning Time As an Adaptive Design Variable in Concept Learning Using Computer Based Instruction." <u>Journal of Educational Psychology</u> 76 (1984): 452-465.

Discussion of process and concept development in computer-based instruction.

1016. ______, R. Park, and D.L. Christenson. "Adaptive Control of Learning Time and Content Sequence in Concept Learning Using Computer Based Instruction." <u>Journal of Educational Psychology</u> 77 (1985): 481-491.

1017. Thompson, M.E. "Beyond The Computer: Reading As a Process of Intellectual Development." ERIC ED 236 555, 1983.

1018. Thompson, R.A. "Computer Assisted Reading Instruction Research." Paper presented at the annual meeting of the International Reading Association, Atlanta, May 1984.

1019. Tinker, R., and A. Naiman. Microcomputers in Education: Applications of Microprocessors in the Schools. Cambridge: Technical Education Research Center, 1980.

Ways computers are used in various educational applications.

1020. Torr, O. "Computer Supported Braille Applications." American Annals of the Deaf 124 (1979): 691-695.

Using computers within teaching situations with blind children.

1021. Trifiletti, J.J. "Microcomputers Versus Resource Rooms For LD Students: A Preliminary Investigation of the Effects on Math Skills." Learning Disability Quarterly 7 (1984): 69-76.

Ways computers are used in special education settings.

1022. Trueman, D. "Telidon and Computer Assisted Learning--A Report on the First Experiment Using Telidon for CAL." ERIC ED 235 795, 1981.

1023. Turkle, S. The Second Self: Computers and The Human Spirit. New York: Simon and Schuster, 1984.

Examination of computer uses in a variety of environmental settings and discussion of research findings as applied to these settings.

1024. Tursman, C. "Microcomputers in the Schools." School Administrator 40 (1983): 14-17.

1025. U.S. Office of Technological Assessment. Informational Technology and Its Impact on American Education. Washington, DC: U.S. Government Printing Office, 1982.

Description of American schools and how they are beginning to use computers.

1026. Van Matre, N.H. "Problems In Researching Computer Managed Instruction." Paper presented at the annual meeting of the American Educational Research Association, Toronto, March 1978.

1027. Von Feldt, J.R. "A National Survey on the Use of Computer Assisted Instruction in Schools for the Deaf." Journal of Educational Technology Systems 7 (1978): 29-38.

1028. Wagschal, P. "A Last Chance for Computers in the Schools?" Phi Delta Kappan 66 (1984): 251-254.

Discussion of panacea effect of computers and their inability to deliver what their supporters promised.

1029. Walker, D.F. "Reflections on the Educational Potential and Limitations Of Microcomputers." Phi Delta Kappan 65 (1983): 103-107.

Essay on how computers are currently being used in schools and rationale for instructional and administrative changes that could increase their effectiveness.

1030. Walker, R.A. "Problems in Researching Learner Control." Paper presented at the annual meeting of the American Educational Research Association, Toronto, March 1978.

1031. Wall, S.M., and N.E. Taylor. "Using Interactive Computer Programs in Teaching Higher Conceptual Skills: An Approach to Instruction in Writing." Educational Technology 22 (1982): 13-17.

Development of writing and higher cognitive thinking skills.

1032. Wangberg, E.G. "Directions and Developments In Micro-comptuer Applications in Schools." Clearing House 58 (1985): 384-386.

New uses of computers in schools including data base and data management techniques.

1033. Ward, R.D., and A.B. Rostron. "Computer Assisted Learning for the Hearing Impaired: An Interactive Written Language Environment." Volta Review 85 (1983): 346-352.

Language development for the hearing impaired using computer technology.

1034. Ware, M.C., and M.F. Stuck. "Sex-Role Messages Vis-A-Vis Microcomputer Use: A Look at the Pictures." Sex Roles 13 (1985): 205-214.

Male and female use of computers and the effects on learning.

1035. Watson,, N.R. Microcomputers in Education: Uses for the `80s. Tempe, AZ: Arizona State University, Department of Elementary Education, 1982.

1036. Waugh, M.L. "Proposed Directions for Research in Computer Based Education." Paper presented at the annual meeting of the National Association for Research in Science Teaching, French Lick, IN, April 1985.

1037. Way, J.W. "Evaluation of Computer Assisted Instruction." ERIC ED 257 1984.

1038. Webb, N.M. "Microcomputer Learning in Small Groups: Cognitive Requirements and Group Processes." Journal of Educational Psychology 76 (1984): 1076-1088.

Using computers in small group instruction.

1039. ______. "Cognitive Requirements of Learning Computer Programming In Group and Individual Settings." AEDS Journal 18 (1985): 183-194.

Learning needs in developing computer programming for individuals and groups.

1040. Weir, S. "LOGO: A Learning Environment for the Severely Handicapped." Journal of Special Education Technology 5 (1982): 20-22.

Use of LOGO for teaching with special education students.

1041. Weizenbaum, J. Computer Power and Human Reason. San Francisco, CA: W.H. Freeman, 1976.

Classic work on the effects of computers and technology on the social and reasoning aspects of societal development.

1042. White, C. "The Impact of Structured Activities with a Computer-Based File-Management Program on Selected Information Processing Skills." Ph.D. dissertation. Indiana University, 1986.

1043. White, D., and L. Rampy. Solutions Unlimited: Delphi Study on Policy Issues in the Introduction and Management of Computers in the Classroom. Bloomington, IN: Agency for Instructional Television, 1983.

Long-range study of ways computers are used and managed in classroom situations.

1044. White, M.A. "Synthesis of Research on Electronic Learning." Educational Leadership 40 (1983): 13-15.

Overview of research studies measuring effectiveness of computer technology.

1045. Wholeben, B.E. "Criterion Standards for Evaluating Computer Simulation Courseware." Paper presented at the annual meeting of the International Society for Educational Planning, New Orleans, October 1984.

1046. Wiechers, G. "Introducing CAI for Developing Nations." Technological Horizons in Education 8 (1981): 39-41.

Use of CAI in a number of educational systems in underdeveloped and developing nations.

1047. Wilkinson, G.L. Media in Instruction: Sixty Years of Research. Washington, DC: Association for Educational Communications and Technology, 1980.

Segment on history of computers in education as part of media instruction.

1048. Williams, F., V. Williams, and A.F. Phillips. "Perspectives on Courseware." Children and Microcomputers: Research on the Newest Medium. Edited by M. Chen and W. Paisley. Beverly Hills, CA: Sage, 1985.

Effect courseware has on children, how its developed, evaluated and implemented.

1049. Williams, G.L. "The Effectiveness of Computer Assisted Instruction and Its Relationship to Selected Learning

Style Elements." Ph.D. dissertation. North Texas State University, 1984.

1050. Wirth, P.A. "Instructional Technology Needs in Rural Special Education." Paper presented at the annual Research In Action Conference, Lubbock, February, 1983.

1051. Withrow, F.B. "Learning Technology and the Hearing Impaired." Volta Review 83 (1981): 263-268.

Effectiveness of computers with the hearing impaired.

1052. Withrow, M. "Computer Animation and Language Instruction." American Annals of the Deaf 123 (1978): 723-725.

Use of pictures in computer technology and deaf children.

1053. Wobble, G.G. "Process and Processor: Is There Room for a Machine in the English Classroom?" English Journal 73 (1984): 34-37.

Analysis of the ways computer technology and word processing software are used in the teaching of English.

1054. Wood, D., H. Wood, and D. Middleton. "An Experimental Evaluation of Four Face-To-Face Teaching Strategies." International Journal of Behavioral Development 1 (1978): 131-147.

Computer technology as an individual learning strategy.

1055. Woodward, A. "The Adequacy of Microcomputer Courseware Teachers Guides." Paper presented at the annual meeting of the American Educational Research Association, New Orleans, April 1984.

1056. _____. "Evaluating the Evaluators: A Study of the Evaluators and Evaluations of Educational Software." Paper presented at the annual meeting of the American Educational Research Association, Chicago, April 1985.

1057. Wright, A. Microcomputers in the Schools: New Directions for British Columbia. Victoria, British Columbia: British Columbia Department of Education, 1980.

Uses of computers in British Columbia. Assessment of successes and plans for new uses throughout all levels of schooling.

1058. Wright, B.D., and M.H. Stone. Measurement as an Instrument of Learning. Washington, DC: National Institute of Education, 1983.

Uses of computers in measuring learning outcomes and in evaluation sequences.

1059. Wright, D.A., A. Melmed, and E. Farris. Instructional Use of Computers in Public Schools. Washington, DC: National Center for Educational Statistics, 1984.

Statistical analysis of computer usage, methods, and place in the curriculum.

1060. Yates, D.S. "In Defense of CAI: Is Drill and Practice a Dirty Word?" Curriculum Review 22 (1983): 55-57.

Effective uses of drill and practice as a computer instructional device.

1061. Zakariya, S.B. "The Computer Goes to School." Principal 61 (1982): 16-20, 52-54.

Administrative uses of computers in a variety of settings.

1062. Zarraga, M.N., and S. Bates. "Computer Time Tabling and Curriculum Planning." Educational Research 22 (1980): 107-120.

Ways to use computers in curriculum planning.

1063. Zucker, A. "Computers in Education: National Policy in the USA." European Journal of Education 17 (1982): 395-410.

A look at computers in the United States from a European viewpoint.

1064. _____. "The Computer in the School—A Case Study." Phi Delta Kappan 63 (1982): 317-319.

Discussion of computer usage in a school from implementation to evaluation.

AUTHOR INDEX

SUBJECT INDEX